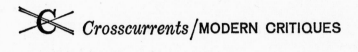
Crosscurrents/MODERN CRITIQUES

Crosscurrents/MODERN CRITIQUES

Harry T. Moore, *General Editor*

The Fiction of Stephen Crane

Donald B. Gibson

WITH A PREFACE BY

Harry T. Moore

SOUTHERN ILLINOIS UNIVERSITY PRESS
Carbondale and Edwardsville

FEFFER & SIMONS, INC.
London and Amsterdam

To J.G., F.C.G., O.J.G. *and* H.H.W.

Preface

Donald B. Gibson's book is another indication of the continuing interest in Stephen Crane, and it is a valuable addition to Crane studies because of its definition of his attitudes—an essential investigation of his vision—and because it is among other things a technical study.

"The continuing interest in Stephen Crane"—he has always been with us, despite a period of comparative neglect, but it is only in recent years that he has become a figure of stature. Critics now see him as one of the first of the "modern" American writers.

A generation ago, when Crane was somewhat neglected, Ernest Hemingway could speak of him, in The Green Hills of Africa (1935), as one of America's "good" writers: "The good writers are Henry James, Stephen Crane, and Mark Twain. That's not the order they're good in. There is no order for good writers." Hemingway's judgments were often whimsical, as his omission of Melville and Whitman shows, but this particular judgment was going in the right direction in that it paid some heed to the true importance of Crane.

But what is this true importance of Crane? Robert Wooster Stallman, who has written most frequently and most usefully about him, began an Introduction to The Red Badge of Courage with the statement, "I think the most important thing to say about Stephen Crane is that he is a great stylist. He puts language to poetic use, which is to use it reflexively and symbolically." Elsewhere Mr. Stallman has noted, and the emphasis is his, "The works

that employ this reflexive and symbolic language constitute what is permanent of Crane."

In the present book Mr. Gibson notes how Crane establishes "a rhythmic pattern of action" in The Sullivan
County Sketches; and Mr. Gibson quotes the openings
of two of them to illustrate what he means. This method
could be extended to much of Crane's significant work.
His openings are famous, particularly the first sentence
of "The Open Boat": "None of them knew the colour of
the sky." The beginning of The Red Badge of Courage
is also well known: "The cold passed reluctantly from the
earth, and the retiring fogs revealed an army stretched
out on the hills, resting." The first sentence of "The Blue
Hotel" has also been widely commented on, especially the
striking use of the word declare: "The palace hotel at
Fort Romper was painted a light blue, a shade that is on
the legs of a kind of heron, causing the bird to declare its
position against any background." Even the less-known
works, such as the novella George's Mother, have these
highly colored, strong-rhythmed openings, and in this
case the entire first paragraph is given in order to provide
a fuller idea of Crane's stylistic strength:

> In the swirling raid that came at dusk the broad avenue
> glistened with that deep bluish tint which is so widely
> condemned when it is put into pictures. There were long
> rows of shops whose fronts shone with full, golden light.
> Here and there, from druggists' windows or from the red
> street-lamps that indicated the presence of fire-alarm boxes,
> a flare of uncertain, wavering crimson was thrown upon
> the wet pavements.

This has very much the effect of an Edward Hopper
painting of an American city street at night. And until
Crane exhausted his talent and his health, he was usually
able to produce such pictures; and they were organic to
his stories.

This somewhat technical discussion has gone on to
such length for several reasons. One of them is that it
shows one of the reasons for Crane's importance and
durability. His writing is all the more forceful in an age

of flat prose, when so many of our younger writers use language merely because they have to, and continually turn out what might be called a grocery-list prose. This was not the case with such successors to Crane as Hemingway, Faulkner, and Fitzgerald: they "wrote," to use the word in quotation marks as T. S. Eliot and Edmund Wilson have employed it in trying to avoid that tricky word style, which so often suggests mere contrivance.

I have also discussed technique because Mr. Gibson does. He is not one of those critics who write literary criticism in a purely conceptual manner, dealing with novels and stories as if their expressional qualities were nonexistent. (How different from the customary criticism of music and painting, which is never purely conceptual.) Mr. Gibson carefully examines Crane's technique, and it is interesting to note the "stylistic" flaws he finds in The Red Badge of Courage. But he also examines Crane's themes and his ideas, for example in a fine discussion of "the final meaning" of The Red Badge of Courage, in which Mr. Gibson finds a duality. By investigating the various versions of the novel, Mr. Gibson is able to discover the difference "between the novel Crane actually wrote and the one he wished to present to the public. Clearly they are not the same."

But Mr. Gibson makes many other contributions, among them his discussion of the influence of Darwin on Stephen Crane. He also discusses Crane's rather unusual deficiencies in reading. Mr. Gibson points out that although Crane was not a systematic thinker, he dealt with many of the great problems which confront us today. Mr. Gibson gives Crane his deservedly high rank, but he does not fail to see his flaws, particularly in relation to what he calls tone, meaning Crane's attitude to his material. Mr. Gibson is at his critical best in just such discussions, and this book greatly increases our awareness of Crane's failures and achievements.

HARRY T. MOORE

Southern Illinois University
April 6, 1968

Acknowledgments

The author thanks the following for permission to quote from the writings of Stephen Crane or to reprint his own published materials: Holt, Rinehart and Winston, Inc., *The Red Badge of Courage and Selected Prose and Poetry* by Stephen Crane (Rinehart Edition), William M. Gibson, editor; Alfred A. Knopf, Inc., *The Work of Stephen Crane* by Wilson Follett (1926) and *Stephen Crane: An Omnibus* by Robert Wooster Stallman (1952); New York University Press, and Peter Owen, Ltd. *The Letters of Stephen Crane*, Robert Wooster Stallman and Lillian Gilkes, editors, and *The War Dispatches of Stephen Crane*, Robert Wooster Stallman and E. R. Hageman, editors; Syracuse University Press, *The Sullivan County Sketches of Stephen Crane*, Melvin Schoberlin, editor; *The Explicator*, "The Red Badge of Courage," XXIV (February 1966), Item 49; University of Texas Press and *Texas Studies in Literature and Language*, "'The Blue Hotel' and the Ideal of Human Courage," VI (Autumn 1964), 388–97.

Contents

Introduction

The recent work (since 1950) of John Berryman, Robert W. Stallman, Daniel Hoffman, Lillian Gilkes, Edwin Cady, and Eric Solomon on the life and work of Stephen Crane has served to stimulate and sustain interest in a writer who contributed significantly to the development of modern American literature. Between the time of the publication of Berryman's critical biography and the present a large body of criticism of Crane's work has evolved, some of it contributing greatly to our understanding of his work. However, it seems to me that generally this body of criticism suffers from a defect common to a great deal of modern criticism, its unconcern with rendering aesthetic judgments. When value judgments are made, they are likely to be no more than adulatory ones, which do not go far in helping the reader to evaluate Crane's work in itself or in relation to other American writers. An outstanding example to the contrary is John Shroeder's early PMLA article "Stephen Crane Embattled." [1] But noting the response to his attack on Crane, we find that most replies recognize little or no merit in his argument, implying that no serious difficulties exist in the conception and execution of *The Red Badge of Courage*.

In their great concern with explication critics have been loath to point out those things in Crane's fiction which even his most sympathetic readers are likely during the privacy of reading to find embarrassing, irritating, or both.[2] Often we allow our desire to define content and structure in an author's fiction to obscure his limitations.

In Crane's work it is worthwhile to observe his shortcomings, perhaps more so than in the case of other authors. The nonevaluative study of his material often suggests that it is better than it actually is. Too, it obscures the fact that his fiction is markedly uneven, his good work being very good, but his bad work, of which there is a great deal, being very bad. I have on occasion found that the flaws in his works bear on meaning so directly that it is impossible to understand thoroughly several major works without exploring the nature of their shortcomings. And finally, only by discovering his weaknesses are we in a position to evaluate his strengths. This should suggest that my interest in calling attention to the less successful aspects of Crane's work stems not from a desire to diminish his stature, but from the desire to understand and evaluate his fiction as best I can.

A number of the defects we find in his fiction are the result of Crane's inability to control his tone adequately, and by "tone" I mean the attitude of the author toward his materials as implied therein. This problem arises first in *The Sullivan County Sketches* and then in several other works, chief among which are *Maggie*, *The Red Badge*, and "The Blue Hotel." Often Crane's tone has a damaging effect on both style and theme, accounting directly in some cases for those stylistic deficiencies marring so much of his best work, compounding the problems to be found in his worst. At other times the tone is perfectly well determined, its utilization being a great asset rather than a liability.

I have found certain insights derived from depth psychology to be useful in describing Crane's conception and treatment of the hero in his fiction. By no means, however, have I used a mythological method of any kind in my study of his work. Rather, I have abstracted from a work by Erich Neumann entitled *The Origins and History of Consciousness* [3] some elements which seem to go far in describing the activities and aspirations of Crane's heroes. In this book Neumann develops in great detail certain of the insights put forth earlier by Jung. I am sure that by choosing certain elements of Neumann's system of thought and neglecting others I have oversimplified and thus distorted his total view. Consequently he should be absolved of any responsibility for the use to which I have put his thought.

The Origins and History of Consciousness has at its base the thesis that the consciousness of modern man, like his body, has evolved through a series of stages. The history of consciousness is recorded in mythology, where we may see first of all the undeveloped ego contained within what Neumann calls the "uroboros," a womblike state, being warmed, nourished, and protected, free from anxieties. The paradisiacal state of the undeveloped ego exists because it is unable to exercise any of the functions of consciousness, chief among which is making distinctions between itself and its surroundings. As the feeble ego becomes capable of distinguishing between itself and the world it gains strength, eventually becoming strong enough to attempt to separate itself from the uroboros. The uroboric stage is maternal in character, and signifies "an historical period in which man's dependence on the earth and nature is at its greatest."[4] Consequently the separation which the ego attempts is at once a separation from a matriarchal sphere and from dependence on nature. Success in the attempt means the establishment of consciousness strong enough to balance the uroboros; failure means death: immersion into nonconsciousness. Separation from the uroboral situation means overcoming it by "slaying" the mother and the father, the representatives of the primordial state, which is represented in myth as the slaying of the dragon. The unsuccessful hero is himself devoured, thrust back into the realm of darkness. If he slays the dragon, the hero is rewarded with treasure of some kind, gold or precious jewels, a fair maiden. His treasure symbolizes his transformation, his achievement of higher consciousness, entitling him to function autonomously in the world.[5]

The foregoing indicates the extent to which I have been influenced by a considerably more complex system of thought.[6] I assume, as Neumann does, that the patterns outlined in the myth correspond to stages undergone by

individuals during the process of the development of consciousness. I find it useful to look at Crane's heroes in this
light.

Though Crane undoubtedly was not aware of the construct through which I view his protagonists, his conception of the hero invites a comparison with fairy tale and
mythology.[7] Often throughout his fiction his characters
view themselves as heroes of myth or fairy-tale, seeing an
analogy between their situations and those of such others.
"The little man" of *The Sullivan County Sketches* sometimes believes that he is a knight or a soldier. Henry
Fleming describes the opposing forces as dragons, and
their flag becomes at one point "a craved treasure of
mythology." George Kelcey of *George's Mother* and
Rufus Coleman of *Active Service* likewise see themselves
as knights having some great task to perform. Such references are not simply few and scattered; they and similar
ones occur quite frequently, suggesting that a composite
hero drawn from Crane's knowledge of myth and fairy
tale underlay his conception of the hero.

The attention Crane gave to the hero in his fiction
bears directly on the problem of his relation to naturalism.
Many critics who have dealt specifically with the subject
have concluded that Crane is a naturalist. By "naturalist"
they mean one who believes that man is as much a part of
nature as all else in the world, and as a part of nature, he
is subject to the same laws and rules governing all phenomena in the universe. In the following pages I attempt
to show that this definition of naturalism does not strictly
apply to Crane. He wrote in this sense only one clearly
naturalistic piece of fiction, *Maggie*, his first novel. Here-
after, there are no places, at least as I read the fiction,
which suggest that man exercises no control over his fate.
We see characters who have only limited control, but the
most thoroughgoing believer in free will admits that the
area of existence over which man exercises control is a very
limited area.

There is the overwhelming evidence in Crane's fiction
that man, through the exercise of consciousness, can separate himself from nature, responding in a manner dif-

ferent from that prescribed by nature. His response can be other than instinctive. Before consciousness is sufficiently strong, one is manipulated by his environment; but when consciousness becomes sufficiently strong, one becomes the manipulator, and, like the hero of myth and fairy-tale, rises above nature. After *The Red Badge,* where certain qualifications need be made, the problem of determinism in Crane's fiction does not arise.

Crane was a naturalist in that he believed that God does not interfere in the affairs of men, and as a result man is left to make of himself and his world what he can. Though the implications of this belief occurred to him (witness the extent to which he carried them in *Maggie*), he found those implications unsatisfactory for reasons outlined in my chapter on *The Red Badge of Courage.* Thereafter, he lost concern for the logical conclusion of his view of God's role in relation to the universe, a response not surprising from one as little inclined toward philosophical speculation as Crane.

In the same way that we must avoid coming to Crane predisposed toward the view that he is a determinist, we should likewise resist the temptation to regard him as a symbolist. For the most part he is no more a symbolist than one must be who uses language, a symbolic medium. His work is like *The Iliad* or *The Odyssey* wherein everything seeks to be clear and open. His works, like those, usually assume the nature of language to be such that one can say what he means, without resorting to the complexities of symbolism. Of course we could read *The Iliad* and *The Odyssey* symbolically, but hardly without the feeling that we were dealing with a kind of symbolism universal in nature rather than a kind generated out of the necessity arising from the requirements of a particular set of relationships. Most of the symbolism in Crane's work is universal and unconscious. Often what has been taken for symbolism is no more than the thing itself. We are generally closer to the truth of Crane's way of looking at things when we interpret literally.

Obviously the problem is no simple one. We see instances in certain pieces, "The Blue Hotel" and "The

Open Boat" being prime examples, where Crane has quite obviously intended the reader to interpret symbolically. But even in these tales it would seem that some limitations should be put on symbolic reading. One should question, for instance, whether water is symbolic in a tale about the sea. One might also consider whether a particular symbolic reading contributes toward some over-all meaning, whether it leads anywhere. A reader familiar with the body of Crane's work will probably—if he approaches the matter reasonably—be aware that the majority of his pieces are nonsymbolic. If he desires to see Crane honestly, he will scrutinize each case thoroughly, being as true as he possibly can to his sensitivity as a reader. This is the most that any of us can hope to do.

I have intended in this study to evaluate the work of Crane and interpret it as one who has long been an admirer of his fiction, but who from the beginning of his experience with him has been constantly aware that all was not right with his fiction. Often, in the privacy of my own mind, I have felt uncomfortable reading Crane, feeling that with few exceptions his fiction seemed just to miss the mark. At the same time I have been constantly aware that Crane achieved certain effects that no one had achieved before him, as well as some achieved by none since. There is a greatness about him which places him far above most of his contemporaries, a certain combination of qualities allowing him to transcend his time in a way that his contemporaries—James and Twain excepted—do not. Yet there remains the specter, the sense of unfulfilled potential which I nearly always get from him. My intention has been to be true to both these responses, to discover his limitations while never losing sight of his strengths. Only by approaching him in this way, I feel, can we know his meaning to us and his relation to our time.

DONALD B. GIBSON

University of Connecticut
December 1, 1967

The Fiction of Stephen Crane

Crane in the Woods

The Sullivan County Sketches are Crane's earliest published fiction. They probably were not completed before
Maggie was, but for our purposes here we will do well to
begin with them since they prefigure (in a way that *Maggie* does not) the major interests, problems, and techniques which Crane was later to employ. The *Sketches* are
more typical of Crane, being more of a piece with the later
work than *Maggie* is, in theme if not in style and tone.
This becomes clear if we recall only a few minor ways in
which *Maggie* differs from the other fiction. The protagonist is a woman; she is completely passive, acted upon, not
acting; she has no awareness of the nature of her difficulty,
not the least self-awareness; her problem is a social problem, whereas in other cases involving society Crane's primary concern is with the active opposition of the individual to society, not with society itself, or even with the
influence of society on the individual.

The *Sketches* are ironic, humorous, whimsical in style
and tone, apparently little more than wild fantasies directed toward an audience not necessarily concerned with
serious fiction. They were indeed written for such an
audience, most of them having appeared in the New York
Tribune in 1892. Nevertheless they treat what turned out
to be the burden of the corpus of Crane's writing.[1] They
explore the individual in crisis and attempt thereby to
define the meaning and significance of self in relation to
nature, other people and ultimately—by implication even
in these slight works—the universe.

Apart from a common setting there are a number of unifying elements in these tales which suggest why Crane himself desired at one time to collect them in one volume. The same characters take part in them; one character, "the little man," is always the protagonist. All of the sketches involve fear on the part of the protagonist or the other characters, of either mutilation or death.[2] But in most cases the fear is either unjustified by the actual facts of the situation or is completely out of proportion to those facts. Perhaps most important for our purposes is the rhythmic pattern of action which Crane establishes in these tales. Each begins with either a brief description of setting ("There was a ceaseless rumble in the air as the heavy raindrops battered upon the laurel thickets and the matted moss and haggard rocks beneath"),[3] or a statement telling the occasion of the tale ("Four men once upon a time went into the wilderness seeking for pickerel"). From thence we move to a fear-inspiring conflict during which the reactions of the characters are studied, and finally to a comic resolution. Whether the concluding movement is indeed comic (as opposed to tragic) is one way of stating one of the central problems of the *Sketches* and will be dealt with through the course of this chapter.

If we take into account the nature of the events themselves, the forest settings of the sketches assume import beyond being merely the locale in which the events of the stories transpire. Most of the plots have to do with the supernatural, or at least what the characters interpret as supernatural. Of course in myth and literature the forest often appears as the primeval forest in which the strange and supernatural exist, and Crane's forests are mysterious, magical places where miraculous transformations can occur. Each tale involves a trial, a test of the protagonist. The forest is the testing ground where initiates prove their ability to survive unaided by the community or by the comforts, conveniences, the safety of the town. But if we compare the danger present in these forests with that existing in the forests of *The Red Badge* or in "A Mystery of Heroism," we see that these sketches seem mere fantasies. And of course they are fantasies, though perhaps not *mere* fantasies.

It is quite fitting that "Four Men in a Cave" should have been the first of *The Sullivan County Sketches* to be published since it appears to be, on one level, a story about birth. The underlying meaning of the symbolic journey into a hole in a hill, through a dark narrow passage to an inner chamber, and the eventual expulsion through a crack in the wall seems to me to need no amplification. But what does require explanation is the meaning of the journey.

As I said previously, all of the sketches involve fear on the part of the four men, especially the hero, the little man, of mutilation or death. Crane apparently feels that fear stems from the insufficiently developed consciousness, the consciousness incapable of exercising control over its environment, of manipulating the environment through the assertion of will. Consciousness is sufficiently developed when the individual becomes the manipulator rather than the manipulated, when he ceases to see himself as an object whose very existence is dependent upon external forces over which he has no control. Fear is overcome, Crane seems to feel, by the assertion of will in opposition to the objects of fear. The ability to face the object of fear manifests the strengthening consciousness; the inability manifests the undeveloped consciousness, or nonconsciousness. "Four Men in a Cave" is a humorous but serious tale about the necessity of conscious development in order to see and respond to the world as it actually is rather than as it is imagined to be.

The four men in the tale have no willed response to the events besetting them; they are manipulated by external forces. In retreating into the cave,[4] the men seek protection from potential destruction by a hostile world. (The degree of fearfulness shown by these men suggests that they are fearful of many things.) They retreat into an area which will supposedly protect, nourish, and sustain them. But they only discover that the retreat into the cave (correlated by Crane to a womblike state because in the womb there are no fear-inspiring objects, people, or situations except to the consciousness far enough developed to view nonconsciousness as threatening to it) constitutes a death which is as frightening, as dreadful as any physical death in the outside world. Nonconsciousness they discover is not satisfying either. The hermit in the tale points to the crevice in the wall and commands them to be gone, to enter the world, to be born again. The voice is an interior voice in each of the men which commands that consciousness attempt to overcome that which threatens it in the world, for only through opposition to antagonistic forces can consciousness strengthen itself sufficiently to allow the individual to function well in the world, to discover, to create identity. Looking ahead for a moment, we may clearly see the meaning of "Four Men in a Cave" by comparing it with the forest chapel scene in *The Red Badge*. There too, the forest retreat which should offer peace, safety, tranquillity, shelter from the attack of literally threatening forces, contains at its center a dead and decaying soldier, a horror different from the horror which Henry Fleming has "escaped." Psychologically the dead soldier serves the same function as the hermit in the sketch, for the sight of death in the womb turns Henry back toward the world. The tale is the prototype of the scene in the novel.

"Four Men in a Cave" leads us to the very center of Crane's major thematic concern and to the central problem of a great deal of his fiction. The resolution of the tale is a feeble attempt to deny the implications of the preceding action. The four men and we as well are supposed to laugh the whole thing off, to dissipate an illusion of fear. But the truth of the matter is that the events of the story would have been interpreted in the same manner by the four men if the hermit had indeed been a "ghoul," a "vampire," a "Druid before the sacrifice," or an "Aztec witch doctor." As a result of this ending, the problem of the tale is not completely resolved. Only on the surface level is there resolution when the men learn the hermit's identity. The deeper problem which the tale poses, the problem of the insufficiently developed consciousness, is not resolved at all; there is nothing to be laughed about on that level. Hence the last section of the tale is antithetical to the preceding events. Crane attempts here to camouflage, to dismiss as fantasy, as error, or as simply comic what turned out to be his primary concern: the insufficiently developed consciousness of the individual confronted by forces hostile to its aims and aspirations, and thus bent on its destruction.

"The Octopush" (octopus), the second of *The Sullivan County Sketches* in Melvin Schoberlin's edition, is one of the least artistically contrived of *The Sullivan County Sketches*. In the other stories there is a clearly defined antagonist who threatens to maim or mutilate the little man or his friends. In this story a vague, undefined, entirely subjective fear having no objective embodiment threatens all of the characters in the story, even the antagonist himself. Hence the power which the role of the antagonist may possess is dissipated by the failure on Crane's part to create a fear-inspiring object so as to motivate and focus properly the fear of the four men.

But with the preceding tale as background we can see easily why Crane insisted upon the element of fear even though he was unable to embody it sufficiently well within the context of "The Octopush." Fear must be met and dealt with, and as the other tales tell us, it can only be dealt with if it emanates from some objective cause. In the third of the sketches the little man is confronted with actual antagonists.

By means of the rather scanty plot of "A Ghoul's Accountant" Crane goes to great lengths to explore the reactions of the little man to the events which befall him. We are made quite aware of the fact that he loses control of his body. "He grew gray and could not move his legs." He staggers blindly to where the "ghoul" directs him. "Foam drifted to his mouth, and his eyes glowed with a blue light." His "blood turned to salt. His eyes began to decay and refused to do their office." "A throe of fear passed over him, and he sank limp in his chair." The continuing concern with bodily control in Crane's fiction is first explored at length in "A Ghoul's Accountant." The matter arises in "Four Men in a Cave," though its implications are not fully realized.

"A Ghoul's Accountant" implies clearly that one of the primary functions of consciousness is to govern the action of the individual. The ability to act under stress in a conscious manner is one of the characteristics separating men from beasts. In reacting as he does the little man in some sense forsakes his humanity, for he is completely at the mercy of his instincts. The most general implication of course is that consciously controlled action is more desirable than nonrational action if one is to realize as fully as possible his potential as a human being. The little man must conquer himself in order to function meaningfully and effectively in the world. It is for this reason that Schoberlin's contention that "a collaboration of natural events, or Nature—naturalism, if you will . . . determines the fate of the little man and his companions" [5] does not seem entirely true. We will see quite clearly that he is potentially capable of controlling his destiny in large measure, but that he must first make some adjustments within himself.

The point of view of "A Ghoul's Accountant" is well managed generally though there are some problems arising in connection with it. The tale is related entirely from the vantage point of the little man. The character who takes him to the old house is referred to as "intruder" or "man" until the little man awakens. Only then is he called "the ghoul," indicating of course that the protagonist rather than the author sees the intruder as a ghoul. But the author participates in a rather unfair way when he implies that the intruder is some kind of devil (his skin is fiercely red, his whiskers infinitely black, and he carries a "pitch-fork") and that nature itself shrinks from him. By informing us in his own person (before the little man awakens) that in the intruder's presence "the campfire threw up two lurid arms and, quivering, expired" and that "the voices of the trees grew hoarse and frightened," he says in effect

that the little man's interpretation of the events that
follow is the correct interpretation, for if nature did indeed respond as the author informs us that it did, then the
intruder is in fact some demon from the lower regions.
The same problem arises with the second sentence of the
story: "The music of the wind in the trees is songs of
loneliness, hymns of abandonment, and lays of the ab-
sence of things congenial and alive." This description is
obviously subjective, yet it is presented as the truth, the
observation of any observer of the scene. Then is the
author taken in just as the protagonist is? No, but he
pretends to be. And he fosters this pretense in order to
make his ironical ending more surprising than it might be
if we suspected all along that the little man were deluding
himself.

The ironical ending itself raises the same thematic com-
plications that the ending of "Four Men in a Cave" raises.
Again the failure is a failure of tone and is reflected in the
problem of the point of view. Certainly an author need
not indicate at the beginning of a work what the outcome
will be, but at the same time he ought not to arrange his
materials so as to preclude or to make unlikely his resolution of the action. Crane tells us that the little man is
involved in a rather serious problem while saying in the
same breath that the problem is not serious after all. The
antagonists are not ghouls or demons from the underworld. So be it. But if they are not, then Crane, the
author, should not tell us otherwise, as he does. We may
smile or even laugh when the wild, gray man kicks the
little man out of the door, yet we cannot help but feel
that some major action has not been resolved. As in "Four
Men in a Cave" the little man's reactions would have
been the same had these actually been supernatural
events. The protagonist is apparently exactly in the same
position that he was in at the beginning of the tale. No
new awareness has occurred.

"The Black Dog," the fourth of the *Sketches* in Schoberlin's collection seems to me to be the most artfully
contrived of the tales so far considered. The protagonist

learns something during the course of the action, and the ironic ending functions beyond the surface level of meaning. Again the tale is about the employment of will in order to control and understand one's fate. At the very beginning we are made aware of the possibility of the little man coming to grips with whatever problem may confront him and perhaps emerging victoriously. It is he who leads his companions through the forest when they have lost their way. Though lost, tired, wet, "menaced" by darkness, "the little man had determination in his legs." [6] He spots the house where they take refuge, clearing the way through the thickets. He "boldly confronted the weird glances from the crannies of the cabin." Yet in spite of his apparent fearlessness, the confrontation with the specter is no simple matter. When he first hears of the black dog, he moves his legs nervously after having seen "night making a million shadows." He continually glances behind his chair while the group listens for the howl. "God!" he screams on hearing the dog's howl. He falls away gasping at the actual sight of the specter. The other characters are contrasted with the little man. They (we only see two of the four companions though the other two are undoubtedly present) completely lose control of their minds and bodies. The "pudgy man" crouches in a corner, "chattering insanely"; the slate-colored man "in his fear, crooked his legs and looked like a hideous Chinese idol"; his old uncle "was turned to stone." Only the little man is capable of rousing himself to action, running to the window first to see the specter, then to hurl objects at it. When the "phantom" ceases to cry, the men, the little man included, "sank limply against the walls, with the unearthly wail still ringing in their ears and the fear unfaded from their eyes." It is at this point that the little man "felt his nerves vibrate," consciously deciding that "destruction was better than another wait," and went to the window to discover what was the thing outside. Crane's attempt to supply motivation for the little man's actions by saying, "In the final struggle, terror will fight the inevitable," is not satisfactory since the other men were at least as terrified as the hero. Here the little man who has all along expressed disbelief in the existence of phantoms, has his opinion confirmed, thereby learning something about the world. He further learns that one need not be paralyzed by external forces which seem overwhelming, that the individual can assert will in a universe which threatens his destruction from time to time, and that problems can be solved by conscious effort.

The ending of "The Black Dog" may seem antithetical to the apparent intention of the tale if it is regarded as a fulfillment of the prophecy made by the slate-colored man early in the story: "He [the black dog] haunts these parts, he does, an' when people are goin' to die, he comes and sets and howls." To be sure, when prophecies of such a specific nature are fulfilled there are usually universal forces at work. But I do not feel that Crane intended this to be suggested by his ending. The old man is meant to contrast with the little man. He is literally frightened to death, perhaps because his illness has weakened him; perhaps he would have died anyway under the stress of the situation. In any case his death suggests the price to be paid for the unwillingness to face the unknown, the fear of facing the unknown, of facing squarely that which threatens to overcome one physically or psychologically. For there is a kind of death involved when consciousness is incapable of manipulating its environment in order to achieve the aims and aspirations of the individual. One defines himself, Crane says, through his actions. One in fact creates himself. We are not unduly surprised by the ironic ending since the old man's throat gurgled and his mouth frothed at the beginning of this last scene. We may be a bit taken aback by the juxtaposition of the fact of the old man's death and the elation which the characters feel when their fears are allayed and the tension relaxed. On the bed the old man lies dead. Outside the dog wags its tail.

Like "The Black Dog," "Killing His Bear" has as its main concern the efficacy of conscious control over self in order to control rather than to be controlled by circumstances and environment. It is a tale of struggle and achievement. The struggle is largely an internal struggle and its result is projected in the successful outcome of the encounter with the bear. There are forces to be overcome if the hero is to accomplish this end. The little man must deal with the tendency toward inertia of his "dumb and bloodless" body, "frozen to a statue." He had been standing in one spot in the icy cold for a long time and his undoubtedly numb body must be willed into his action. As the bear nears, he grows tremendously excited. This nervous energy must be channeled into carefully controlled motion. When the bear finally breaks through the thicket, the little man stands "like an image" until he comes within range of the rifle. Then the hero slowly changes his aim with "a wee motion, made with steady nerves and a soundless swaying of the rifle barrel." The little man aims at a spot under the foreshoulder.

> The earth faded to nothing. Only space and the game, the aim and hunter. Mad emotions, powerful to rock worlds, hurled through the little man, but did not shake the tiniest nerve.
> When the rifle cracked, it shook his soul to a profound depth. Creation rocked and the bear stumbled.

Here again, as in "The Black Dog," the little man by dint of will maintains control in a stress situation. Only a highly developed consciousness could cope with the forces which urge flight, which oppose consciously directed activity.

Crane goes to great lengths to indicate to the reader that there is more involved here than the scant plot line would suggest. All through the tale are references to blood, battle, and death. "On the ridge-top a dismal choir of hemlocks crooned over one that had fallen." The sun is a "dying sun" and its beams are "crimson beams." The little man's blood swims or throbs or surges in his veins. The cry of the hound at first has "bloodthirstiness" in it, and "his baying tells of the approach of death." "The yell of the hound grew until it smote the little man like a call to battle." The baying of the hound grows "bloodcurdling." The setting sun finally fades "to a dull red splash," throwing "a faint timid beam of a kindred shade on the snow." And when the bear is shot "blood was oozing from a wound under the shoulder, and the snow about was sprinkled with blood." The implications of these references suggest the scope of the action taking place in "Killing His Bear" as well as indicate again, as is implied in "The Black Dog," that a penalty is exacted if conscious will is not utilized and thus strengthened. Too, there is a ritualistic aspect of the tale. The little man is involved in a test of endurance. He pictures himself "in a thousand attitudes under a thousand combinations of circumstances, killing a thousand bears" because this particular test, like any test, provides a *representation* of ability. Killing his bear successfully should suggest the capability of dealing with any number of problems which require the employment of consciousness against forces which seek to overwhelm it and the individual. Just as in the tale the little man's power to direct his conscious energy is so great that when he prepares to fire his rifle "the earth faded to nothing" and "only space and the game, the aim and the hunter" existed, so beyond the tale he is apparently equipped to manipulate his environment to the degree necessary for survival in the worst human situations that may occur.

"Killing His Bear" was the last of *The Sullivan County Sketches* to be published in the *Tribune*. It is impossible to tell whether their order of publication was arranged by Crane, whether indeed the whole of the sketches was conceived with some sort of structural pattern underlying them. His plan to collect the sketches in one volume never came to fruition. Whatever the case may be in actuality, whether Crane or some editor decided on the order of the sketches, there does seem to be a rather clearly defined movement from "Four Men in a Cave," the first sketch, to "Killing His Bear." In the last sketch the hero is obviously considerably more mature, more capable of dealing with experience in an effective manner than the ineffectual hero of the first three sketches. The little man in "The Black Dog" is more manipulating than manipulated, though even there he does not achieve the apogee of control of mind and body. "Killing His Bear" is an unambiguous account of the hero's state of being after having progressed from a lower to a higher state of consciousness.

A definite break does occur after this last story. Here the little man regresses to the state in which we found him at the beginning of the tales. We cannot know whether Crane intended the cyclical movement which this suggests since the next tale, "An Explosion of Seven Babies," was not reprinted during Crane's lifetime.

What is most interesting about "An Explosion of Seven Babies" is an underlying fairy-tale motif which appears later in *The Red Badge*. As in the earlier tales the point of this one is that the little man is insufficiently prepared to deal with the situation in which he finds himself, and as a result he is the powerless victim of himself, as well as his antagonist. But here he is the unsuccessful hero of the fairy-tale who otherwise encounters the hostile beast, dragon, giant, seeks to overcome it and is rewarded for victory over his opponent with gold, a princess, magical powers, or some other symbol of a more highly developed consciousness. At the beginning of the tale the little man is lost in the forest, a typical fairy-tale situation, when he comes to the high wall. Then he confronts the "brown giantess," who crouches, snarls, and roars like a beast, "like a dragon." "Some bellowing animal," observes the pudgy man, "seemed to have his friend in its claws." Unlike David, who slew his giant, and unlike Jack, the Giant Killer, our hero retires defeated, gaining no reward, no kingship, no golden egg-laying goose. "I wish she hadn't called me a beast," he observes, revealing a submerged feeling of inadequacy as a human being.

Since Crane uses the third person limited point of view in this tale, it is impossible to tell whether the events described are actually of such magnitude (how much of a giantess was this brown sunburned woman?) But that does not matter. The little man views himself as the hero of myth and legend who encounters and should over-whelm the apparently stronger opponent, but who fails.

It is also relevant that our hero is confronted by a *giantess* rather than a *giant*, and that the encounter takes place within the walled-in area. The forces which hinder the development of consciousness are often interpreted as feminine in nature. Frequently the influence of mothers is seen as attempting to thwart the development toward individuality of sons in order to maintain the role of nourisher and protector. Such is the case in Crane's *George's Mother*, which has this problem as its central concern.

The beast or dragon, however, is not *simply* symbolic of the mother, but it represents all those forces inimical to the hero's development. Chief among these forces is fear. Thus we may interpret nearly all of *The Sullivan County Sketches* in such terms. In some cases more than others ("An Explosion of Seven Babies" is one) Crane seems to invite this mythological interpretation. I would not insist upon this interpretation nearly as much in this story as in "Four Men in a Cave," where, it seems to me, the cave may clearly be seen as a womb. The walled-in area where the little man's agon occurs in "An Explosion of Seven Babies" suggests the same ground.

Again as in the earlier stories the little man is terror-stricken. And again Crane describes the condition of his legs in order to inform the reader of his terror: ". . . trepidation showed in his legs." He loses control of his body: "He felt his blood begin to dry up and his muscles turn to paste." The pudgy man is equally afraid. After falling over the wall and seeing the giantess turn to the attack, he "quaked miserably and yelled an unintelligible explanation or apology or prayer." When the little man discovers him crouching in the forest after the encounter his eyes are "terror-gleaming." The significance of this fear is clear enough.

Aside from the obvious meanings involving the hero's reaction to fear which "A Tent in Agony" contains, there

are two significant matters worth our regard. One is that
though the bear wins in this tale, he himself falls victim to
a circumstance which to him is as frightening as was his
appearance to the little man. After extricating himself
from the tent, "He cast one disheveled and agonized look
at the white thing, and then started wildly for the inner
recesses of the forest." The implication to the little man
of the bear's predicament is that this "monster" is not so
terrible after all. He goes "into giggling hysterics" when he
sees the bear entangled because he sees that this thing
which frightened him nearly out of his wits has limitations
just as he does. In this sense "the devil made a twin," and
his realization allows him to repose by the campfire calmly
smoking.

The other matter is the symbolic use of fire in this tale.
The light of the fire is the light of consciousness, of
understanding, of reason, as opposed to the darkness of
fear and nonconsciousness. When the bear appears, the
little man is encouraging "his companion, the campfire"
and puffing "fiercely" at his pipe. The bear steps out of
darkness into the light, challenging the hero's claim to the
light of consciousness. When the hero's fortunes are at
their lowest ebb, after he has climbed the tree, crying, and
he "moans a speech meant for prayer" and clings "convul-
sively to the bending branches," when he is in darkness,
his conscious powers completely inoperative, he gazes
"with tearful wistfulness at where his comrade, the
campfire, was giving dying flickers and crackles." The
embers merely glow. But after he achieves the realization
that the bear itself is indeed not "the unknown" or the
unknowable, as he had thought at the beginning of the
tale when he first becomes aware of its approach, he is
able to rebuild the fire and to puff "pompously" on the
pipe which he had of course dropped. To be sure, that
rebuilt fire is a bright one, and that pipe glows as never
before, since prior to this experience he had not "confronted the terrible."

"The Cry of Huckleberry Pudding" does not succeed as
well as some of the other tales. It lacks the economy of

focus of those tales in which the little man, as the central character, performs the main action. Crane has a problem in this tale which he is not able to manage successfully. Since the little man acts in the interests of the antagonist, it becomes necessary to create a new protagonist, but rather than make one of the other three men the protagonist, Crane attempts to describe the reaction of the group of men, emphasizing the part of the pudgy man by having him be the major spokesman. But we do not know the pudgy man as we do the little man, and because the pudgy man has no distinct character apart from the others, we do not respond to him as to the little man whom we have come to know through the course of the tales. Though the pudgy man is the only one of the three identified by appellation, he merely voices the response of the group. His fears are the particularized fears of the group; there is no distinction between his reactions and those of the two shadowy characters who accompany him.

But a more significant cause of failure seems to me that "The Cry of Huckleberry Pudding" is simply not interesting, partly because we learn nothing new either about the little man or his companions. Worth observing also is the fact that in the total context of the tales the little man is the center of interest, and since the tales are so slight anyway, we have little concern for the fate of the other characters since they mean so little to us.

From the very beginning of "The Holler Tree" the pudgy man is the protector of the eggs he carries along the forest path. He goes to great lengths to see that they are not broken. But the point of the tale is that the egg must be broken, that the hero must emerge from the womb if he is going to be capable of performing significant action in the world, as the chicken emerges from its womb, the eggshell. The eggs serve as a symbolic comment about the pudgy man. He is incapable of heroic action, content to function ineffectually, within the confines of his infantile consciousness. Before the hero can function, before he can slay a single dragon, he must have developed a level of consciousness sufficient to allow the submission of himself to danger and to the possibility of the total annihilation of consciousness, of his own body. The little man's unconcern for the eggs, the pudgy man's great concern for them, both comment upon the character of the men as well as symbolize the essential problem of the hero.

When the little man sees the hollow tree, he immediately sees as his goal the attainment of its so-called "treasures." Thus the motif of quest. There would seem to be little danger in climbing a hollow tree, but Crane makes it quite clear that the accomplishment of the hero's end is neither safe nor without great difficulty. Several times he nearly falls. Pausing at one point to talk to the men below, he almost loses his grip and "it was near being fatal." Reaching the top, the hero gazes around and is able to see a great deal farther than his companion below. Heroes can. The little man hesitates once he has gained the top of the tree, for the hole is dark and "it looks pretty dangerous." When the pudgy man taunts him with being afraid, he conquers his fear for the moment, lowering himself partially into the hole. He hesitates once more. Taunted again, he raises his fist to protest, but disappears down the hollow passage. His companions are "fearful he had met his time" because he is now in the very maw of the dragon where he must either prove himself or be extinguished. The second phase of the drama occurs here.

The little man, captive within the hollow tree, begins to rage against the pudgy man as the cause of his being in his predicament. The "furious quarrel" which develops between them represents the conflict which we have seen as the second phase of all the tales so far. This conflict is the objectification in a realistic story of the agon occurring between the hero and the forces which seek to impede the development of consciousness. Thus the pudgy man represents the element to overcome.

Our hero is able both to defeat his antagonist and to free himself by his own powers at the same time. Violently angry, he simply is enabled by vigorous movement to upset the tree. "It seemed like a mighty blow aimed by the wrathful little man at the head of the fleeing pudgy man," who having fled for his life, lies "white with terror," trembling.

By dint of his feat, the little man has brought about the conditions necessary for his rebirth into the world, a wiser and more powerful being. Unlike most childbirths, the birth of the little man occurs feet first. When he comes forth from his womb, he is "of deep bronze hue from the coating of wet dead wood." (Blood and amniotic fluid?) He feels his shoulders and legs, then rubs "the crumbles from his eyes." He is a new man. He observes the pudgy man for a moment; a smile is "*born* at the corners of his mouth." (My emphasis) "There's your eggs—under the tree," says he to the pudgy man, indicating the central concern of the story, to break the egg, to hatch. His consciousness of the significance of his action, as well as his awareness of success are indicated in the last line of the tale: "His stride was that of a proud grenadier." And it should well be if we remember the outcome of the somewhat similar tale, "Four Men in a Cave." Here he succeeds.

In "Four Men in a Cave" the little man is motivated to explore the cave because "its black mouth had gaped at him." In "The Mesmeric Mountain," the last of the *Sketches*, his motivation is not very different. The "irregular black opening in the green wall of forest" beckons to him in much the same manner. He is a curious little man and is always anxious to explore the unknown, seeking, though he is not fully aware of what it is that he seeks. Not knowing what the door of the forest leads to, he is sure that it will lead him to "some discovery or something." The urge for quest which he has is largely below the level of rationality; it is a prompting emanating from the very depths of his psyche. And as we will see later on, the urge to strengthen consciousness by pitting oneself against superior forces cannot be easily suppressed. The little man simply cannot avoid the contest between him and the mountain.

While he is gazing at "an irregular black opening in the green wall of forest," the little man sees a rabbit come out from a thicket and sit there. He throws a rock at it; the rabbit runs through the opening, and the "shadowy portals" of the forest seem to the little man to close behind him. This vignette is a miniature presentation of the essential problem of the hero. We saw Crane use the device in "The Holler Tree," and we will see it again in the forest scene in *The Red Badge* when Henry Fleming throws the pine cone at the squirrel. The response of the rabbit to the fear-producing stimulus indicates a rather basic mode of response, one in which consciousness does not come into play. Man, because he is different from the lower animals, is potentially able to respond in various ways to a fear-inspiring situation. But the potential of consciousness is not always realized, and when it is not, man falls victim to all those things in experience which in any way threaten him mentally, emotionally, or physically. The little man must endure the trial awaiting him in the wilderness in order to know what his capabilities and limitations are. As we have seen from the above summary of the plot of "The Mesmeric Mountain," the little man's first response to the threat of the mountain is exactly parallel to the response of the rabbit when he is threatened by the stone. The problem of the hero is to discover whether he is capable of acting otherwise.

I will not insist that the womb symbol which I believe is clearly evident in "Four Men in a Cave" and "The Holler Tree" occurs here, though the "irregular black opening" and the references to it as a door suggest a different world from that outside. We would expect anything that had portals which close behind one to be containing, as the womb is containing. But let it suffice to say that the forest is a world apart, perhaps a kind of magic forest even, where the possibility of transformation exists. When the little man passes "from the noise of the sunshine to the gloom of the woods," we are made explicitly aware that this forest is no ordinary wood. After him "the green portals closed, shutting out live things," and he trudges on, conscious of his aloneness.

In the depths of the forest, after having climbed the

pine tree in order to get his bearings, the little man attempts to avoid the challenge of the mountain by changing his course away from it. To have been able to do so, would have been to deny the promptings which sent him into the wilderness in the first place. The whole point of the undertaking would have been forsaken and at the end of the story he would be the same man that he was before he entered the forest. But what else other than some overpowering unconscious drive could have forced him to confront the mountain, though twice he changes his course away from it? He is, after all, an experienced woodsman, and therefore not likely to have traveled in circles as might an inexperienced person. The implication of his inability to escape the mountain is that once consciousness is sufficiently strong to translate into action the unconscious promptings toward the quest, once the journey has been undertaken, the agon cannot be avoided. The hero may succeed or he may fail, but the trial will take place.

The price of failure in this tale is death. The mountain threatens to crush the little man's head, thereby suggesting not only his physical death, but the extinction, or perhaps more accurately, the arresting of conscious development. So the little man attacks the mountain, exposing himself to its wrath, to its "granite arm" which is ever ready to smite. Gaining the summit, he earns the right to swagger "with valor" as he does. He has conquered the mountain; it is "motionless" under his feet. And by implication, he will now be more capable of controlling his own destiny.

A minor theme of "The Mesmeric Mountain" is that nature seems actively to oppose the ends of man. This theme, though not dealt with in the preceding pages, occurs throughout *The Sullivan County Sketches*, as well as throughout a great deal of Crane's subsequent fiction, notably *The Red Badge*. Here in "The Mesmeric Mountain" grass and trees seem to obstruct the little man; stones cut his shoes; he battles "ignorant bushes"; "dark-green laurel" opposes him. Such references occur prominently in nearly all of the sketches. They have to do with man's being a part of nature. Since nature and its processes are nonconscious forces, they apparently oppose conscious activity, for in developing his consciousness to a degree higher than that of anything else in nature, the hero views nature as an active adversary, though in reality it cannot be since in itself it completely lacks the least degree of consciousness of man or of his ends. The task of the hero is to escape from his natural self, so to him it only *seems* that nature is actively hostile.

The concern with external nature in Crane's fiction is not essentially different from his concern with natural processes and their role in the hero's development of consciousness. In "Killing His Bear" the hero must direct a great deal of energy toward overcoming by means of dint or will the natural processes which apparently seek to render him helpless. His body is "dumb" and "lifeless" because it has succumbed to some degree to these natural laws involving the lowering of temperature by coldness, the circulation of the blood, the glandular reactions occurring with fear or excitement. "The Mesmeric Mountain" shows us the little man at a time when his "legs are about to shrivel up and drop off." Fatigued, cold, or afraid, the hero must utilize his will in order to perform whatever task is before him. He must dissociate himself from nature.[7]

"The Mesmeric Mountain" differs from not only all of *The Sullivan County Sketches*, but from everything else that Crane wrote. Unlike the rest of the fiction, this story is pure fantasy. Although the events in several of the tales are rather improbable, they are not impossible. It is quite unlikely that a bear would become entangled in a tent as in "A Tent in Agony," but we are willing to grant the fictional possibility of such an occurrence. In "The Mesmeric Mountain" Crane does not attempt to establish verisimilitude in the central action of the tale. This might well be attributable to Crane's emotional inability at this point in his career to expose his hero to the imminent possibility of actual death. Another reason might be that

Crane did not wish to interfere with the light, rather whimsical surface tone of the tales.

The central problem of most of *The Sullivan County Sketches* is their tone, Crane's attitude toward his materials. We do not object to the chasm separating the surface level of the action from the more serious level; obviously there is nothing wrong with dealing with serious matters in a humorous way. But we might very well object when the two levels are at odds, when one level contradicts the other. And this is what we find in these sketches. In most of them the characters, especially the little man, are treated with devastating irony, the implication being that their fears are groundless, and they are fools to fear those things they fear. But at the same time, Crane also says that their problem, the development of consciousness, is a problem common to all men, and he treats this problem with seriousness. But if we are confronted with a serious and meaningful problem, then can we accept it as serious and meaningful when the characters embodying it, working it out through their actions, are merely fools? The little man has been referred to as a supreme egotist whom we are supposed to laugh at. But how can we accept the apparent cynicism of the ending of "Killing His Bear" ("Upon his face was the smile of the successful lover") when we have developed such a high degree of identification with the hero through the course of the narrative? Or how can we laugh very deeply about the ironical endings which indicate that the men had nothing to fear, when we know that their reactions would have been the same whether they had faced real threats or simply imaginary ones? Crane seems to have been unable to decide whether the problem of the men was indeed a meaningful problem, or whether it should have been seriously treated at all.

The Sullivan County Sketches define what was to develop into one of Crane's major concerns, the possibility of heroic action. Can man be free enough from the forces inimical to his being to accomplish significant action in the world, to determine his own fate to any degree? In spite of the difficulty involved in freedom from the limitations imposed by man's being biologically an animal, man can free himself. This is Crane's answer to the question in *The Sullivan County Sketches*. In *Maggie* Crane answered the question negatively. In that world man is entirely governed by the laws of nature. The sketches showed us certain forces that were antagonistic to man's aspirations to separate himself from nature, and thereby define some central core of self. *Maggie* shows us other forces, forces which have demonstrated the futility of any effort on the part of man to escape from his animality. These Crane discovered in Darwin.

2

Crane Among the Darwinians

I know of no evidence even remotely suggesting that Crane derived the terms of Darwinism directly from Darwin's work.[1] On the contrary, we will be on fairly sure ground if we infer that Crane indeed did not read Darwin since it is quite certain that he read very few books of any kind. Even his most sympathetic critics do not extend themselves very far in saying what books he might have read. Berryman makes the greatest claims in stating as fact (though obviously merely speculation) that Crane knew Tolstoy, Flaubert, Shakespeare, "a crowd of authors English and American whom he disliked," the English Bible, Emerson, Whitman, Twain, Kipling, and Poe.[2] I doubt seriously that he knew any of these authors very well, and of them all I would speculate that he knew the Bible best. If he did *know* these authors in any meaningful sense, he certainly went to great lengths to conceal the fact. And if his knowledge was shaky here in the area of his greatest interest, how much more so must it have been in regard to peripheral concerns.

It would not have been the least bit difficult for Crane to have absorbed passively the knowledge of Darwinism evinced in his work. By the 1890's, even semiliterate persons would have known something about Darwinism,[3] just as today everyone knows something about atomic energy. As early as 1873, only thirteen years after the publication of the *Origin of Species* in this country, the following observation about the widespread popularization of Darwinism could be made in a popular magazine.

The Taine of the twentieth century who shall study the literature of the nineteenth, will note an epochal earmark. He will discover a universal drenching of belles-lettres with science and sociology, while the ultimate, dominant tinge in our era he will observe to be Darwinism. Not only does all physical research take color from the new theory, but the doctrine sends its pervasive hues through poetry, novels, history. A brisk reaction discovers its presence in theology. Journalism is dyed so deeply with it that the favorite logic of the leading article is "survival of the fittest," and the favorite jest is sexual selection. In the last new book, in the next new book, you will detect it.[4]

Large numbers of books were published whose primary purpose was to explain evolution to the average educated person in nontechnical terms. A glance at any one of the major popular journals of the later nineteenth century, *Arena* (circulation over one hundred thousand), *Popular Science Monthly, North American Review*, will indicate something of the extent of the general curiosity about Darwinism. Volumes and volumes of words were spoken during public lectures and sermons when experts and laymen, clergymen and secular speakers aired opinions of every kind, attacking, defending, finding new areas of application, discussing old areas, all serving to disseminate Darwin's message throughout the land.[5]

Crane's intention in *Maggie, A Girl of the Streets* was neither to support nor to refute Darwinism as he understood it. Rather, his central concern was in railing against the nature of things, raging against the universe which Darwin describes, but raging against it as one might rage against the daily rising of the sun. He accepted the Darwinian scheme so far as he understood it, with no question as to its truth or its adequacy for defining the life situation.[6]

Maggie manifests a considerable change in attitude from that apparent in *The Sullivan County Sketches*. In the earlier work there is at least the possibility of free action, action resulting from a decision on the part of a character. But in *Maggie* no such possibility exists. Even if we decide that the little man does not actually perform heroic action, we yet must grant that he is not determined in his actions. No one in *Maggie* is free.[7]

The hypothesis of Darwin, unless qualified, leads the artist into a morass of inconsistency and contradiction, a morass from which young Stephen Crane was unable to extract himself. *Maggie*, Crane inscribed in one copy of the book, ". . . tries to show that environment is a tremendous thing and shapes lives regardless." [8] Crane carries this idea to its extreme by making his characters "nothing but" animals, apparently not recognizing that in so doing he relinquishes his prerogative as author to judge them. If Maggie is simply a victim of her environment, then so are all of the other characters and so is the rest of society. Nobody is to blame for anything and we cannot help but cringe when Crane attempts with irony to condemn Maggie's fellow victims.

If we consider the matter closely enough, then it becomes obvious that on the ideational level the tale is entirely inadequate. For not only has Crane surrendered his right to judge, he has likewise denied this right to the reader. Unless the reader is sufficiently wary, then he too will fall into the inconsistency inherent in the conception of the book. He will find himself judging characters who have absolutely no responsibility for their shortcomings nor, indeed, for any virtues that they might have.

It should be recognized in all fairness that Crane did not intend that we examine too closely the implications of his premises. Continuing the inscription cited above, Crane wrote, "If one proves that theory [the influence of environment upon the individual], one makes room in heaven for all sorts of souls, notably an occasional street girl, who are not confidently expected to be there by many excellent people." Crane obviously intended to elicit sympathy for Maggie, though at the expense of the other characters in the novel who, all together, represent the whole of society. The inadequacy of the basic conception of the tale becomes even more apparent when we note that the terms of Crane's statement, without reservation, tell us that there is room in heaven not only for Maggie, but for her lover, Pete, her brother, Jimmie, and her reprehensible, repugnant, disgusting mother, Mrs. Johnson. But Crane, becoming subject to the very same shortcoming which he criticizes in others, is not willing to "make room in heaven" (whatever that means) for the other characters. Hence, the disparity occurring between his achievement and his intention in *Maggie* emerges when we compare his statement of intention with his actual accomplishment. The inconsistency indicated by such a comparison, and the ramifications of the basic error in conception reveal in large measure why the book is less than a first-rate work of art.

The severe irony with which the characters are treated exists because Crane renders judgment of his characters through that means though he cannot legitimately do so, at least according to his initial assumptions. But even if we overlook the contradiction, we can see without great difficulty that Crane's irony betrays him in other ways. Because the characters, Maggie included, are treated with such devastating irony, the reader is likely to find it difficult to involve his sympathies with anyone in the story.[9] Aside from Maggie herself there is only one other character in the story who could conceivably elicit the least bit of sympathy, Jimmie, Maggie's brother. From time to time he has a flickering awareness that he should not judge Maggie so harshly. But such awareness only flickers weakly, so weakly in fact that when Maggie returns home he joins Mrs. Johnson in driving her from the apartment. " 'Well, now, yer a t'ing, ain' yeh?' he said, his lips curling in scorn. Radiant virtue sat upon his brow, and his repelling hands expressed horror of contamination." [10] Ironically—the irony here is too explicit to be a reasonable approximation of the illusion of reality, a matter to be discussed later—Jimmie has only a few moments before told Hattie, a girl who bears the same relationship to him that Maggie bears to Pete, "Oh, go teh blazes!" Jimmie cannot engage our sympathies for long.

In responding positively to Maggie, we are likely to be responding to an idea rather than to a seemingly live character.[11] Since Maggie is so deficient in knowledge, intelligence, judgment, sensibility, even common sense, she has only her simplicity to recommend her to us. She is beautiful we are told, but we never *see* her beauty; she is supposedly kind, but since we never see any evidence of her kindness except in her youth, there is no reason to believe that she is any more kind than the vegetable which is incapable of either good or evil. What we are intended to see is the most simple and innocent humanity at the mercy of predatory beasts. What reader with the least reading experience can become seriously involved with a conflict between these cruel, vicious, animalistic people and Maggie, who "blossomed in a mud-puddle," and had "none of the dirt of Rum Alley . . . in her veins"? The sympathy we have for Maggie is little more than that which we could have for *any* helpless person or animal overwhelmed by devastating forces. Crane elicits a stock response. In treating Maggie with such irony—especially in dwelling on her completely inadequate ability to cope with the simplest life problems—he compounds his failure to create a sympathetic character. He might have shown us her deficiencies without the irony, without seeming himself to scorn her.[12]

But Crane scorned her because he found it impossible to like any of the characters in his work very well. In forgetting through the course of the work that his statement, ". . . environment is a tremendous thing and frequently shapes lives regardless" applies to everyone in the book, he reverted to the feelings that prompted a sentiment he expressed in a letter in 1896, "The root of bowery life is a sort of cowardice." [13] What has seemed to some critics to be "objectivity" or "ironic detachment" is not that at all, but loathing and disgust for the depraved characters of whom he writes.[14]

Crane's attitude toward his characters created a conflict between what he wanted to say in *Maggie* and what he found himself saying through the course of the work. His irony betrayed him to the extent that Maggie herself

appeared just as crude and unattractive as the other characters. Crane, either consciously or unconsciously, dealt
with this problem in a rather simple way. In order to
differentiate Maggie from the other characters in the story
he gradually withdrew her from participation in the events
of the narrative. Her character is not revealed in action as
are the characters of the other major participants; she
seldom speaks directly as do others. Between the eighth
chapter and the last, Chapter XIX, Maggie utters only
two sentences, "Dis is outa sight!" (Chapter VIII) and
"I'm going home" (Chapter XIV), which she repeats
once. She leaves home only when coerced by Pete or
ordered out by her mother. Even when she commits sui-
cide, her only act of any consequence in the story, she
seems to be in a somnambulate state, hovering somewhere
above the plot, not in the same context as the other
characters. Maggie's position in the novel is a direct result
of the inconsistency noted above: since there is no "room
in heaven" for the other characters, Maggie must be differentiated from them, though Crane paid the price of
committing the same error that those who wouldn't admit
Maggie to heaven committed.

It is questionable whether the sustained irony of *Maggie* is as successful as it might have been at the hands of a
more experienced Crane. This question too points back
toward the problem of the basic conception of the novel.
When the irony here is most artificial, most contrived, it
seems to intend to point out the baseness of the characters, to censure them further for being the result of their
environment. Usually the irony is overdone to the extent
that it becomes unintentionally humorous, destroying the
illusion of reality. Such is the case when Mrs. Johnson says
of Maggie: "Ah, who would t'ink such a bad girl could
grow up in our family, Jimmie, me son," and when the
mother is outraged by Jimmie's suggestion that Maggie be
returned home: "What! Let 'er come an' sleep under deh
same roof wid her mudder agin? . . . Little did I t'ink
when yehs was a baby playin' about me feet dat ye'd grow
up teh say sech a t'ing teh yer mudder—yer own mudder."

It is a bit difficult to believe that the hypocritical Mrs. Johnson would likely muster such false sentiments. Likewise the final scene where Mrs. Johnson learns of Maggie's death is hardly credible and very humorous.

> "Well," said he, "Mag's dead."
> "What?" said the woman, her mouth filled with bread.
> "Mag's dead," repeated the man.
> "Deh blazes she is!" said the woman. She continued her meal. When she finished her coffee she began to weep.

Though many of the problems of style in *Maggie* are attributable to the inexperience of the author, several of the stylistic deficiencies are directly traceable to the problem of point of view, which is simply another way of referring to the imperfection of the original conception of the story. The great gulf separating the language of the Bowery characters from that of Crane reflects the author's lack of sympathetic involvement with his people. Crane's preference for words of a learned character and for overly formal sentence structure suggests condescension toward the Bowery inhabitants, the distance between the two levels of usage being a measure of the distance between author and subject.

> There came a time, however, when the young men of the vicinity said, "Dat Johnson goil is a putty good looker." About this period her brother remarked to her: "Mag, I'll tell yeh dis! See? Yeh've eeder got t' go on d' toif er go t' work!" Whereupon she went to work, having the feminine aversion to the alternative.

At best Crane's style in *Maggie* is uneven. All too often his meaning is obscured by tortured sentence structure or by vague, imprecise diction. At worst his self-conscious and tortured diction abuses the language, distorting whatever thought he intended to convey.

> The quiet stranger had sprawled very pyrotechnically out on the sidewalk.

> He had an evening dress, a moustache, a chrysanthemum, and a look of *ennui*, all of which he kept carefully under his eye.

There was given to him the charge of a painstaking pair of horses and a large rattling truck.

At last the father pushed a door, and they entered a lighted room in which a large woman was rampant.

He had been in quite a number of miscellaneous fights, and in some general barroom rows that had become known to the police.   ("miscellaneous"?)

There followed in the wake of missiles and fists some unknown prayers, perhaps for death.   ("unknown"?)

From a window of an apartment house that uprose from amid squat ignorant stables there leaned a curious woman.   (What are "ignorant" stables?)

She wore no jewelry and was painted with no apparent paint.   (Was she painted or not?)

Anyone who has paid attention to Crane's style in *Maggie* should be able to recall that there are many other examples of stylistic infelicity which might have been selected. Likewise there are instances in which Crane's sentences are ambiguous, violate common logic, or are unclear because their meaning is incomplete. Such is the case when Crane tells us that ". . . Maggie blossomed in a mud-puddle. She grew to be a most rare and wonderful production of a tenement district, a pretty girl." Surely there is no correlation between social environment and the physical structure of one's face and body. Why is it odd that a pretty girl should be produced in a tenement district? Crane also tells us that Maggie worked ". . . turning out collars with a name which might have been noted for its irrelevancy to anything connected with collars." Aside from the fact that this statement is not relevant to its context or to the context of the novel, it suggests that there should necessarily be some relationship between collars and their brand names. Even if the name of the collar is entirely unrelated to the collar itself, what is the point? Another stylistic problem in *Maggie* involves the metaphors and similies throughout the book. As is the case with much of the diction, the figures of speech represent attempts on Crane's part to get beyond the barriers of traditional literary style and though sometimes his unusual comparisons are effective, most often they seem merely peculiar and do not go very far in conveying a clear, sharp image or in revealing a new or more meaningful way of seeing objects. Usually when Crane's metaphors fail in *Maggie* it is because the vehicle is not within the realm of ordinary experience and thus the reader finds it difficult to establish the relationship between tenor and vehicle. When he does establish the relationship, it is only after having gone through much effort, having created for himself an image which Crane only suggests.

His wan features looked like those of a tiny insane demon.   (Who has seen "a tiny insane demon"?)

The babe sat on the floor watching the scene, his face in contortions like that of a woman at a tragedy.   (Do women contort their faces at tragedies more so than men? If so, in what way do they contort their faces?)

Her bare red arms were thrown out above her head in an attitude of exhaustion, something, mayhap like that of a sated villain.   ("Sated" with what?)

Pete at intervals gave vent to low, labored hisses that sounded like a desire to kill.   (What does the desire to kill sound like?)

A baby falling down in front of the door wrenched a scream like that of a wounded animal from its mother.   (Even if wounded animals scream, certainly various ones scream differently.)

Overwhelmed by a spasm of drunken adoration, he drew two or three bills from his pocket and, with the trembling fingers of an offering priest, laid them on the table before the woman.   (Do the offering fingers of priests often tremble?)

> In a room a woman sat at a table eating like a fat monk in
> a picture.   (Why "in a picture"? Is this a religious fig-
> ure or a monkey?)

Probably many of these figures were quite meaningful to
Crane; he likely knew very well what he meant when he
compared a woman eating to "a fat monk in a picture."
But whatever response the figure aroused in him remained
private, for I doubt that the image of a fat monk in a
picture has very particularized meaning to most people.

Though most of this commentary has been directed
toward pointing out the shortcomings of Crane's first
novel (a task which has been avoided by other Crane
enthusiasts in spite of the fact that modern tastes, I feel,
are not appealed to greatly by this novel), there are a
number of positive things which might be said about it.
Some of Crane's most successfully created characters appear here. Detestable as they might seem to a reader, Pete,
Jimmie, and Mrs. Johnson are vigorous, living people who
during the course of the novel's action etch out their
characters through violent action, standing out in bold
relief from the amorphous mass of characters who provide
the backdrop for the central events.

We see only the exterior of Pete, but that is all we need
to see for Crane's purposes here. Concerned exclusively
with appearances, Pete dresses in a manner which he
considers elegant, swaggers about in order to impress the
world even further, keeps his bar very neat, and is much
concerned with acting so as not to offend his employer.
The degree of his aggressiveness and hostility precludes
the possibility of sympathy or understanding on his part.
His whole manner has served to shield himself from a
threatening environment.

Jimmie, the only character other than Maggie toward
whom Crane has some measure of sympathy, though
aggressive, hostile, hard, ruthless, has at least the potential
ability to extend sympathy and understanding toward another human being. He considers, if only momentarily,
that there might be some relation between his feelings
about Maggie and the feelings of the brothers of girls

whom he has treated badly. He wonders whether Maggie shouldn't be brought back home, and he has the impulse to rescue his friend after the barroom brawl scene. None of these things would apparently ever occur to Pete. Because he is morally a cut above Pete, Jimmie is not punished at the end of the novel. Pete in his last scene is shown at his most degraded. Completely scorned by his lady love, "the woman of brilliance and audacity," and even robbed by her, Pete is left unconscious from drink. Wine drops softly down upon the blotches on his neck.

Mary Johnson, Maggie's mother, is one of no more than two, in my opinion, memorable female characters created by Crane. If we should forget her, it is likely to be that we have repressed the memory of her as we repress many unpleasant experiences. She has not one redeeming feature. Hypocritical, an alcoholic, incapable of sympathetic involvement with another human being, Mrs. Johnson, red-faced, disheveled, tears through life like a cyclone, destroying anything in her path not strong enough to stand firm. She apparently is the primary cause of the difficulty of the Johnson family. The father, though not one whom most people would wish for a father—or even a relative for that matter—seems prevailed upon by Mrs. Johnson as much as any other member of the family is. He is not on intimate terms with the children, but they have not the same terror of him that they have of their extremely active mother. Like the other main characters, with the exception of Maggie, we know what Mrs. Johnson is by what she does.

Maggie contains a number of scenes which should have indicated to the editors and critics who first saw it that Crane was a talented young writer with a great deal of potential, though sorely in need of experience. I have in mind three scenes: the opening descriptive paragraphs of the beer hall episodes, Chapter VII and XIV; and the fight scene, Chapter XI. Although each of these episodes contains flaws of the kind mentioned above, there is enough effective writing to offset the deficiencies.

Chapters VII and XIV are both attempts to describe,

impressionistically, crowded bowery beer halls. The scenes are intended both to acquaint the reader with one aspect of bowery life and to set the scene of the action to follow. The two chapters begin with a generalized impression, pointing out the details that one might perceive immediately upon entering either of the halls. The second paragraphs describe in greater detail the setting described generally in the first paragraphs. This arrangement suggests the manner in which a viewer might see the scene, first taking in the whole, then gradually becoming aware of and analyzing the general into its particulars. In Chapter VII we are told in the first paragraph that "the place was crowded with people grouped about little tables." The second paragraph interprets the fact: "The vast crowd had an air throughout of having just quitted work. Men with callused hands, and attired in garments that showed the wear of an endless drudging for a living, smoked their pipes contentedly . . ." The remainder of the paragraph goes on to describe in greater detail the composition of the crowd.

Chapter XIV escapes merely repeating the impression conveyed in the earlier chapter though the form, as outlined above, is the same. The latter scene conveys the impression of a larger and noisier crowd, more animated and excited. "The musicians played in intent fury," and the tempo of the music seems "to impart wildness to the half-drunken crowd." Crane does not attempt here to describe the crowd in such detail as he did in Chapter VII. "Shrill voices of women bubbling over with drink-laughter," "plenteous oaths," "rapid chatter" are heard, but they are not assigned to particular people or to particular groups of people. There is not too great dependence on color or on adjectives in general, though beginning authors are likely to rely on these.

The effectiveness of Chapter XI is largely dependent upon the fact that the section constitutes a unit complete unto itself. In itself it forms a little drama, with beginning, middle, and end. As do several other chapters, this one begins with a description of the setting of the action to take place. The setting is a bowery saloon, a rather fancy saloon, "papered in olive and bronze tints of imitation leather," and with "a shining bar of counterfeit massiveness." Behind the bar is "a great mahogany-imitation sideboard reaching to the ceiling," faced with mirrors, and on its shelves glasses, decanters, napkins, and fruits are precisely arranged. In the exact center of the arrangement sits a nickel-plated cash register. Opposite the seeming orderliness of the bar stands a smaller counter which ". . . held a collection of plates upon which swarmed frayed fragments of crackers, slices of boiled ham, dishevelled bits of cheese, and pickles swimming in vinegar." The juxtaposition of the two areas of the barroom, one apparently ordered and the other disordered, reflects the bowery situation in that throughout the tale the seeming order of routine existence is constantly faced with potential disorder, violence, which threatens to erupt at any moment. There is no stability in the bowery, Crane seems to say, and what looks like order and stability is merely counterfeit, imitation. Since disorder is inherent in the bowery situation, no order can be more than ostensible.

What we see at the very beginning of this chapter could very well be a stage setting, the major action of the little drama proceeding out of it.

> At this moment the light bamboo doors at the entrance swung open and crashed against the wall. Jimmie and a companion entered. They swaggered unsteadily but belligerently toward the bar, and looked at Pete with bleared and blinking eyes.
> "Gin," said Jimmie.
> "Gin," said the companion.
> He bent his head sideways as he assiduously polished away with a napkin at the gleaming wood. He wore a look of watchfulness.

At this point the two companions begin to taunt the bartender, baiting him until he comes from behind the bar, confronts them, and eventually strikes out. The argument itself leading up to the brawl indicates quite clearly the growing tension among the combatants. The details of the description of the conflict are as vivid as a reader could hope for.

> They bristled like three roosters. They moved their heads pugnaciously and kept their shoulders braced. The nervous muscles about each mouth twitched with a forced smile of mockery. . . .

The battlers fight an inconclusive battle; it becomes a free-for-all and is soon broken up by a policeman who comes charging down the sidewalk and bouncing through the doors. Jimmie escapes; the other two are being taken to the station.

The only intentional humor in the story is in this scene. A "quiet stranger" orders a "beeh" as Jimmie and his friend burst in. As the antagonism grows between the bartender and his two rivals the quiet man "moved himself and his glass a trifle farther away and maintained an attitude of obliviousness." Then, becoming certain that a fight is going to develop, he moves "modestly toward the door." When the fight begins, he vanishes. Later we see him sprawled "pyrotechnically" on the sidewalk. His rather comic movements punctuate the brisk ferocity of the main action.

This it seems to me is the best chapter in the book, and it succeeds largely because it is dramatic. The certainty with which Crane handles the language indicates a considerably firmer grasp of his materials than in most other episodes: here he *knows* his scene and his characters. Though there are a few lapses in diction, the chapter as a whole seems comparatively well under control.

Underneath the words in which *Maggie* is told can be detected the tone of an outraged man; a man outraged because the nature of things is such that in this world innocence, purity, goodness are not sustained, because these virtues do not arm one in the struggle for survival. No one in the novel, we may assume, is even equal to Maggie in moral stature. Yet it is she who through the working out of the law of the survival of the fittest is annihilated, whereas the less worthwhile creatures survive.

Nature's obliviousness to human values became one of Crane's primary concerns in his later fiction. We see its first expression here.

Others in the latter half of the nineteenth century were interested in the same problem in various ways. In an article in the *Popular Science Monthly*, T. H. Huxley made the following observation:

> If there is a generalization from the facts of human life, which has the assent of thoughtful men in every age and country, it is that the violator of ethical rules constantly escapes the punishment which he deserves; that the wicked flourishes like a green bay tree, while the righteous begs his bread; that the sins of the fathers are visited upon the children; that in the realm of Nature ignorance is punished just as severely as willful wrong. . .[15]

Such attitudes as this contributed greatly to the pessimism current during the time, but more specifically it is not unlikely that Crane's feeling, expressed in *Maggie*, that no benevolent agency seems concerned with protecting the righteous and the just lies at the root of the blasphemy characteristic of much of his poetry. He was never able to reconcile the notion of an ordered universe with his own observation of the working out of events, a problem essentially the same as that of Job and of the Christ who when on the cross falters and asks, "Why hast thou forsaken me?"

In contrast to the sketches about the little man, *Maggie* has at its center a completely passive character, one incapable of dealing with her environment in any manner. The ambivalent attitude expressed by Crane toward such people should perhaps suggest his dissatisfaction with the deterministic scheme. He couldn't accept it nor could he let it go. We will see this conflict being dealt with in subsequent works, and we will note especially how it plays havoc with the author's tone again and again.

3

George's Mother and Other Minor Bowery Works

Before it was entitled *George's Mother* Crane's second novel bore the title *A Woman without Weapons*. Both titles have certain limitations, but the original, while perhaps not significantly better than the final one, reveals more about the content of the book. The word "weapons" implies that the nature of the conflict in the story is such that the woman would fare better were she armed. She is, according to the first title, a defenseless woman. And so in the novel she is. The combat that occurs between mother and son is one she could not hope to win. The most she could hope to do would be to fortify herself morally in order to accept the condition of the mother which usually involves the child's eventual separation from her dominance. In actuality, it seems to me, the mother's problem is not to maintain her position of authority over her son, but rather to develop the inner strength necessary for continuance in a role different from her original role. There comes a time in the life of most men when they must cease to be dependents, and establish their own claims to autonomous existence. *George's Mother* is a story about the conflict that occurs when a certain young man reaches that stage in his life when he feels that he must free himself from parental authority.

At the beginning of the book George Kelcey is returning from work one evening when he runs into an old friend who invites him to have a drink. George has a drink, several in fact, and as a result is much later for supper than he usually is. While George is drinking with his friend, Mrs. Kelcey is cleaning house and cooking supper.

> There was a flurry of battle in this room. Through the clouded dust or steam one could see the thin figure dealing mighty blows. Always her way seemed beset. Her broom was continually poised, lancewise, at dust demons. . . . And as she went on her way her voice was often raised in a long cry, a strange war-chant, a shout of battle and defiance, that rose and fell in harsh screams.[1]

The terms of the description here seem intended to convey some sense of the atmosphere of constant conflict surrounding the bowery inhabitants as well as to characterize the mother-son relationship. The description is misleading in the sense that Mrs. Kelcey is not of a bellicose nature and her weapons and manner of combat are considerably different from those suggested by the description of her furious activity.

After her chores are finished Mrs. Kelcey, nervous because of her son's lateness, moves aimlessly about the flat or sits staring at the clock. Five forty-five, six o'clock, nearly seven, and still George does not come. The stage is set for the first combat we see between George and his mother. Shortly after seven the son arrives. George explains that he ran into Jones and talked with him about old times. "Oh, that Jones," she said. "I don't like him." They sit down to supper. It is here that Mrs. Kelcey is most assertive of her claims on George, but in a way that allowed Crane to think of her at one point as "a woman without weapons." Her method of combat precludes the use of force; she is far more subtle than that. She attempts to bend George to her will by means of subservience. In an obverse way, through a quiet, nonassertive resistance to George's need and desire to establish his own claims as a mature human being, Mrs. Kelcey, prior to the action of the novel and many times in the novel, has been able to maintain dominance over George. She will coax and persuade rather than attempt force. And she is as successful as she is because George himself is not entirely convinced that he is not still a child subject to her authority. Whether one gains one's will through passive means is dependent upon the attitude of the opponent: it is questionable whether Jews in Nazi Germany would have improved their lot by passive resistance, yet India achieved its independence in this way because England felt the injustice of its position. By analogy George recognizes the claims on him of his mother and hence the power of the two opponents is nearly enough equal to allow a struggle whose outcome is uncertain.

Though Mrs. Kelcey knows that George does not always act as she would have him act, she is not actually conscious of the nature of their conflict, nor of the nature of the power she yields. The demands she makes on George stem from her attempt to continue the parent-child relationship. In telling George that he should hang his coat up, that he should eat more, that he should not associate with this or that person, she is simply acting as she has probably acted since George was a child.

The climax of this particular episode, which introduces us to the central problem of the novel, occurs when Mrs. Kelcey asks George to accompany her to church. Though George refuses to go, he is not comfortable about his decision, indicating again his uncertainty about his ability to function autonomously in the world. Mrs. Kelcey, "a woman without weapons," puts her arms about his neck and coaxes him with caresses.

> "Well, now, y' see," he said, quite gently, "I don't wanta go, an' it wouldn't do me no good t' go if I didn't wanta go."
>
> His mother's face swiftly changed. She breathed a huge sigh, the counterpart of ones he had heard upon like occasions. . . . She cast a martyr-like glance upon her son and went mournfully away. She resembled a limited funeral procession.
>
> The young man writhed under it to an extent.

Now that the central problem of the novel has been defined in the first three chapters (the first chapter introduces us to George, who in meeting Jones supplies the immediate motivation for the conflict to occur in chapter three; the second chapter introduces Mrs. Kelcey, showing her long wait for George and her resulting irritation with him; and the third chapter describes the immediate conflict, indicating at the same time the depth of the problem) we have only to see its working out. Will George through the course of the novel establish his own identity? If so, at what cost to himself and to Mrs. Kelcey? Will the desires of Mrs. Kelcey prevail? If so, at what cost to her and to George? Who is the central character in the novel? George, as the nature of the conflict would seem to suggest, or Mrs. Kelcey, who is emphasized in both the original and the later title? These and many other questions we will expect to be resolved through the course of the action of the novel.

Soon after the first conflict between George and his mother, the rift between the two apparently grows greater as George asserts his independence from her by becoming further involved with Jones and a group of other ne'er-do-wells who form a club for the purpose of drinking and having a good time. His first evening with this group George stays out late and gets very drunk. Mrs. Kelcey, who doesn't even know that George drinks, suspects nothing when George arises, irritable, out of sorts because he has a hangover. His temper seeks "something to devour." He would like to attack directly the source of his irritation, which seems beneath the surface to be his mother who "unjustly" woke him up and who has reprimanded him for leaving the light burning all night. His attack is an indirect one, for knowing that Mrs. Kelcey is very much opposed to swearing, he exclaims savagely, "Damn these early hours!" "His mother jumped as if he had flung a missile at her." And of course he would very much have liked to fling a missile at her, but his feelings toward her will not allow him to commit such an overt act of hostility. She asks him to bring home sugar when he returns in the evening. "Yes, if I kin remember it," he replies. By the end of the meal, "The little old woman saw that she had offended her son. . . . She made haste to surrender. "Ain't yeh goin' t' kiss me good-bye?' she asked in a woeful voice." Obviously her "surrender" is no surrender at all, but an attempt to win the fray in a direct though converse way. George kisses her in a deferential and condescending manner.

When he returns from work that evening his spirits have changed completely. He capers around the room; waltzes with his mother; tells jokes, seeming on the whole "to be a lad of ten." After dinner he settles down to smoke his pipe and read the evening paper, commenting to Mrs. Kelcey about the news of the day.

> The week thereafter, too, she was joyous, for he stayed at home each night of it, and was sunny-tempered. She became convinced that she was a perfect mother, rearing a perfect son. There came often a love-light into her eyes. The wrinkled yellow face frequently warmed into a smile of the kind that a maiden bestows upon him who is her first and perhaps last.

This passage, occurring at the end of the fifth chapter, tells us more about the nature of the relationship between George and his mother, foreshadows the probable outcome of the action, and, in relation to what has preceded it, completes the pattern of the action to follow. It restates Mrs. Kelcey's attitude that she and George should remain mother and obedient son, suggesting no awareness on her part that any other relationship is either possible or desirable. Further, we are told that she does not separate, in her feelings at least, this relationship from that existing between man and maid, between lovers. Her motherly love is so all-pervasive that it recognizes no distinctions among varieties of love, and of course such distinction would be necessary for her to make were she ever able to recognize George's claims to separation from her, to individuality in his own right.

The last sentence of the quotation above suggests that some kind of separation is likely to occur, the implications being that the *status quo* will not continue, but that George will take some kind of effective step toward alter-

ing the relationship. He is to her "first" among men and
perhaps her last love (being the last child upon whom she
has been able to maintain a strong hold).

Throughout the novel the lad oscillates between rebellion and childlike acceptance of the relationship between
him and Mrs. Kelcey. This kind of pattern allows Crane a
great deal of freedom in the development of his theme.
He was never given to the organization of tight, well-struc-
tured wholes in his longer works; hence they all tend to be
episodic. *George's Mother* is no exception. Given the
pattern of rebellion and reconciliation, Crane is free to
choose any number of occasions which might serve to
point the conflict between George and his mother. And, as
we might very well expect, the various episodes and groups
of characters have no more than a tangential relation to
each other.

Another manifestation of George's attachment to his
mother, his inability to function as an autonomous individual, is his failure to bring his own self-image into
proper relation to the way things actually are. Out of
motherly affection Mrs. Kelcey believes George to be a far
more worthy person than he actually is. No matter
whether she has actually been responsible for the development of George's image of himself, she is largely responsible for his being unable to see things as they are.

> . . . he often saw that she believed him to be the most
> marvellous young man on earth. He had only to look at
> those two eyes that became lighted with a glow from her
> heart whenever he did some excessively brilliant thing.

As long as George persists in these false notions of self, he
will never be able to discover any kind of meaningful
identity, never be able to come to grips with the world,
establish significant relationships with others.

We learn that George is unable to form satisfactory
attachments to women through Crane's description of
what happens when he becomes enamored of Maggie
Johnson, the central character of the earlier work. Though
the comparison might seem odious to some (justifiably

perhaps) it is instructive to compare George's conception of Maggie to Stephen Dedalus' conceptions of "E. C." and Mercedes in Joyce's *Portrait of the Artist as a Young Man.* There Stephen in his youth is unable (in his mind) to separate "E. C." from the Virgin herself. "E. C." becomes a creature of his imagination, and her great purity and innocence are likely to exist more in Stephen's head than in reality. Mercedes, who is suggested to Stephen by *The Count of Monte Cristo,* likewise partakes of the Virgin-like quality with which Stephen seems to invest all women. They are to him unattainable, spiritual, more ideal than real creatures.[2] Stephen's feelings are mirrored by George. The same idea of womanhood controls the thoughts of both young men, though George is apparently much older than Stephen. Both feel that they will some-day meet in the real world figures corresponding to those in their imaginations.

George gathered from books he read that ". . . there was a goddess in the world whose business it was to wait until he should exchange a glance with her. It became a creed, subtly powerful. . . . Meanwhile he could dream of the indefinite woman and the fragrance of roses that came from her hair." George's fantasies are comparable to those which Stephen has about events like those in *The Count of Monte Cristo.* Maggie becomes his Mercedes. "The shade of this girl was with him continually. With her he built his grand dramas so that he trod in clouds, the matters of his daily life obscured and softened by a mist." George never indicates to Maggie his fond affection.

We are told about George's concern with Maggie in chapter seven. Thereafter the whole matter is dropped from the novel, never to return again. The relationship between George's total psychological state and his view toward women has a thematic relation to the remainder of the book, but like so many other episodes here it fails to cohere beyond the thematic level. It is merely another facet of the total problem existing as a result of the central problem of the book, the problem of discovering one's identity in the face of the conflicting claims of the parent.

How does Crane indicate that this particular involvement is related to the central problem of the novel? I am not sure that he was himself totally aware of the connection between George's abortive concern with Maggie and his conflict with his mother. At the end of the chapter George has become angry because he sees Maggie going out with Pete, the character who seduces Maggie in the earlier novel. Enraged, he explodes when Mrs. Kelcey makes the mistake of nagging him about hanging up his coat. "Don't yeh ever git tired a' hearing me yell at yeh" she says. "Yes," he says angrily, turning "toward his mother a face red, seamed, hard with hate and rage." They stare for a moment, then Mrs. Kelcey turns and staggers from the room. Two explanations occur which would explain George's renewal of open conflict with his mother. One is that he simply transfers his anger toward Pete to his mother who does indeed provoke him. The other possibility is that his anger toward her stems from the dim awareness that she is somehow responsible for his situation. Though we cannot tell from this chapter alone which is the more reasonable explanation, I would suggest that the former is the more correct in view of the fact that every episode in the novel seems to have the purpose of renewing and deepening the growing antagonism between mother and son. In order for this function to be served, it is not at all necessary that George have any awareness of the basis of his problem.

Two additional episodes form the core of *George's Mother.* One involves the associates whom George gains as a result of his contact with Jones at the beginning of the novel; the other has to do with a group of delinquents with whom George becomes involved in the last section of the novel. Both episodes indicate George's attempt to establish some kind of identity in a strange and hostile world. The group which Jones leads him to is composed of men who are older than he, but who offer him no meaningful direction. They are pleasant, cheerful, friendly, but they give him nothing beyond drink and revel. He becomes disenchanted later in the novel when he discovers that their apparent friendship is superficial, that they have no real concern for him though it seems they do at first. After a drunken brawl that keeps him out all night, George returns home with a lie to tell his mother in order to keep the peace. Again he becomes the obedient, dutiful son, "content to read the papers and talk with his mother."

Between this episode and the next in which he joins the group of delinquents George comes again into conflict with Mrs. Kelcey when she repeats her request that he go to "prayer-meetin'" with her. He gently refuses, after which she accuses him of never doing anything she asks. "Whatever am I goin' t' do with yeh?" she asks. "She faced him in a battleful way, her eyes blazing with a sombre light of despairing rage."

> He looked up at her ironically. "I don't know," he said, with calmness. "What are yeh?" He had traced her emotions and seen her fear of his rebellion. He thrust out his legs in the easy scorn of a rapier-bravo. "What are yeh?"
> The little old woman began to weep. . . . He was smitten with a sudden shame. . . . "Well," he said, trying to remove a sulky quality from his voice, "well, if yer bound t' have me go, I s'pose I'll have t' go."

Here the swing of the pendulum widens as George is at once at his most defiant and most conciliatory. Whereas earlier when he refused to go to church he was not aggressively hostile, he now openly defies Mrs. Kelcey, yet capitulates to the extent that he is willing to concede to her wishes.

George goes to church—but the fact of his going to *church* is not so important as is the fact that he makes a concession to Mrs. Kelcey. He commits an act that is most contrary to his will. For this reason it is unimportant whether Crane's sentence, "The little church, pierced would die with a fine illimitable scorn for its slayers" is a direct reference to the crucifixion since it makes no difference in the meaning of the story. We need not consider such implications here nor in *The Red Badge of Courage*, because in neither case does such a reading increase our understanding of the works. Even if such specific references are intended, it is unfortunate, for in each case the references remain isolated, not the least bit integrated into any total frame of reference. To dwell upon the matter of Christian symbolism in either piece is misleading given the outlook governing most of Crane's fiction.[3]

George begins to drink regularly, stay out late, associate with bad companions, and generally to lead a life of dissipation. Mrs. Kelcey is aware that he is worsening, but her reproaches only bring increased rebelliousness. Eventually George begins to associate with a gang of idle young men who gradually influence him by their cynical contempt of life and their sense of its futility. At about this time George and Mrs. Kelcey have their most serious encounter. George, angered because he has to get up in the morning, swears "a tangled mass of oaths." Mrs. Kelcey, knowing "that the momentous occasion had come. It was the time of the critical battle," harshly reprimands George. He swears again, this time at her, and after challenging her to do something about it, takes his hat and leaves. They are silent for three days until George informs his mother that he has lost his job.

The pendulum swings back when Mrs. Kelcey falls ill and George becomes again the dutiful, obedient son. He makes an effort to withdraw from his gang, but is persuaded to have a drink with them. When the drinking is finished, George is drawn into a conflict with another of the members of the gang. Before the conflict is settled he is called away by a little boy who tells him that his mother is ill again. Mrs. Kelcey dies after George's arrival.

Thus the problem of the novel is ostensibly solved, though one might doubt whether in solving the conflict in this way Crane has managed adequately to come to grips with the problem. Having one of the combatants die of natural causes tells us little about the possible range of adjustments that might be made in order that George might establish some kind of autonomy. In all fairness I should point to the possibility that Mrs. Kelcey's death should be read symbolically, as suggesting that in order for George to realize an identity separate from hers it is necessary that she die to him to be resurrected in a new role and in a new relationship to her son. But even if we should give the ending this reading we can hardly allow a symbolic reading to serve the requirements of the literal plot. No matter how we look at it the ending is weak.

Crane believed *George's Mother* to be a very good book, considerably better, in fact, than *Maggie*. William Dean Howells thought the later book superior to *The Red Badge*. Hamlin Garland's estimate is far more accurate: "It will live only as a literary phase of a brilliant young literary man . . ." Garland's judgment is the truer one for several reasons, chief among which is Crane's failure here to realize fully the implications of the problem which he poses. He sets before George the problem of discovering his identity and then condemns him at every turn for trying to come to grips with the problem. Not seeming to understand the necessity of every man's performing the acts or series of acts which will result in his freedom from parental authority and the discovery of his own identity, Crane treats George most unsympathetically. He also fails to see that George cannot discover himself without in some way coming into conflict with Mrs. Kelcey.

On the last page of the novel Crane indicates an awareness that conflicts of interest *do* occur in child-parent relations, but it is not clear whether he realizes that they *must* occur. In the last few lines of the story, just prior to Mrs. Kelcey's death, George overhears a mother in the hall calling her son to go to the store. The little boy tells her to send his sister. She insists that he go. "All right, in a minnet!" he says. "Johnnie!" the mother yells. "In a minnet, I tell yeh!" But in view of the fact that George is treated so unsympathetically during the course of the novel (even his typically adolescent fantasies are ridiculed) it would appear that Crane merely means here that boys are cruel to their mothers, not that a kind of cruelty is inherent in the situation itself.

Garland's feeling that *George's Mother* gives evidence of an inexperienced young author will be borne out by a reading of any section of the novel. Its irony lacks all subtlety, seeming even distasteful at times when it is intended to belittle characters, apparently for the sake of displaying the author's cleverness. Since it is extended throughout the novel and at the same time heavy-handed, it soon becomes tedious. Crane's manner of introducing new characters or events reveals an awkwardness typical of young authors. "One day he met Maggie Johnson on the stairs." "One evening of this period he met Jones." "At a certain time Kelcey discovered that some young men who stood in the cinders between a brick wall and the pavement . . ." "Once in another street Fidsey Corcoran was whipped by a short, heavy man." Infelicities of style are not hard to find: "It could be seen that a great thought was within her." "A pain above his eyebrows was like that from an iron clamp." "Kelcey had that in his throat which was like fur."

Yet there are a number of indications here that Crane's ability as a writer has grown since *Maggie*. I would hesitate to agree with his own statement that *George's Mother* "leaves *Maggie* at the post," yet Crane is in somewhat better control of his materials in the later novel. Although the irony is somewhat clumsy in this work, it better serves Crane's ends than did his irony in *Maggie*. The style in the later work still gives evidence of artistic immaturity, but the phrasing and the diction are considerably better controlled than earlier. On the whole the figures of speech in *George's Mother* are not quite as strained and are more expressive of comprehensible meanings. The central problem of the later novel is a more difficult one to handle since it is primarily an internal, psychological problem rather than one externally imposed by the forces of determinism or by society.[4]

We are not nearly as far from the central thematic concern of *The Sullivan County Sketches* as one might immediately think. The problem of both George and the little man is essentially the same in spite of the fact that the circumstances of each are considerably different. Each must develop and strengthen his consciousness to the extent that he can function autonomously; each must become sufficiently strong not only to discover, but *to have* an identity separate from everything and everybody else in the world. The little man is attempting to free himself from the fear of bodily annihilation; George from domination by parental authority. The little man is slightly advanced in the struggle, for George must first free himself from his original environment before he can go out into the world to test his body. It is worth noting here that Mrs. Kelcey is responsible for George's leaving the scene of the impending fight with Blue Billie near the end of the novel. It is she who thus far has prevented George from coming to grips with the real world.

But is she the central character of the novel, or is George? My analysis would indicate that George is. The title of the novel would indicate that Mrs. Kelcey provides the focus of the work. The problem is complicated by the fact that Crane vascillated between the titles *A Woman Without Weapons* and *George's Mother.*[5] The changes suggest confusion in Crane's own mind about whether the novel was George's or Mrs. Kelcey's. Crane was torn between recognizing as central the most sympathetic character and seeing as central the most active character. Since Mrs. Kelcey is such a passive figure, and since practically all of the book is about what happens to George, I find it hard to see her as the center of focus of the novel. Had Crane not strongly suggested that George was directly responsible for Mrs. Kelcey's death,[6] and had he written with the knowledge that the mother must necessarily alter her role, that she too was to blame for the situation, then the problem would likely not have arisen. We may conclude then that the problem of focus in the novel stems from Crane's original failure to assess adequately the nature and implications of the conflict between the mother and her son. This selfsame failure likewise is responsible for the novel's unsatisfactory tone.

"An Experiment in Misery" and "The Men in the Storm," while of slight literary value, and hardly stories at all in the traditional sense, are nonetheless significant because they reveal one facet of Crane's attitude toward the Bowery and its inhabitants. Interestingly enough, Crane had "An Experiment in Misery" in mind when he wrote to Miss Catherine Harris the statement quoted in part above about the influence of environment on the individual: [7] ". . . I tried to make plain that the root of Bowery life is a sort of cowardice. Perhaps I mean a lack of ambition or to willingly be knocked flat and accept the licking." It is very doubtful in my mind that he achieved this intention in the little sketch.

"An Experiment in Misery" describes an experience that Crane had though it is of course impossible to say just how much of the story is actual fact. The central character of the story is a young man who apparently is just beginning Bowery life. He is not clearly Crane; one would not think to identify Crane closely with the central character did he not know the facts governing the origin of the story. The young man does not know his way around the Bowery, and the story is about his initiation into a basic knowledge of Bowery habitation: where to sleep, where to eat. The story begins late at night and ends the next morning. During the intervening time, the young man finds a free meal at a saloon and with the help of another "outcast" discovers a flophouse where he can sleep for seven cents. A man would have to be very dedicated to discovering the way things are in such a place in order to spend a night in the room Crane describes, especially if he didn't have to. The next morning the two have breakfast, after which they find their way to a park where they sit observing the passers-by. "He confessed himself an outcast, and his eyes from under the lowered rim of his hat began to glance guiltily, wearing the criminal expression that comes with certain convictions." [8]

There is more compassion for his characters in this piece than in most of the Bowery works. If there is criticism leveled against any group of people, it seems directed toward the rest of society, not the denizens of skid row. "The people of the street . . . walked in their good clothes as upon important missions, giving no gaze to the two wanderers seated upon the benches." I see nothing in the story itself which would tend to suggest that "the root of Bowery life is a sort of cowardice." The irony character-istic of the early Crane is present here, but it is more gentle than we might expect, possibly (I won't press the point) because Crane saw more of himself in this story since he was reporting something that might well have happened to him.

In like manner "The Men in the Storm" comes from actual experience. The story is about a group of men who stand in a blizzard waiting to be admitted to a five-cent per night lodginghouse where free coffee and bread are served in the morning. The whole piece, a scenic descrip-tion rather than a narrative, concentrates on the reactions of the men who, cold and anxious for warmth, are impa-tient to get inside. The ending occurs when the men pass into the lodging house out of the storm.

Again what criticism there is here is criticism of society at large rather than of the Bowery element itself. There is first of all a contrast drawn between those who are walking along toward homes and hot dinners and those who must wait out in the storm. There is a man who appears on the scene who suggests the well-fed, well-clothed section of society.

> He was rather stout and very well clothed. His beard was fashioned charmingly after that of the Prince of Wales. He stood in an attitude of magnificent reflection. He slowly stroked his moustache with a certain grandeur of manner, and looked down at the snow-encrusted mob.

Compassion is the keynote here as we are asked to pity these unfortunates many of whom are indeed not regular habitués of flophouses, but are men who at the moment are out of work, who are ". . . men of undoubted pa-tience, industry, and temperance, who, in time of ill-for-tune, do not habitually turn to rail at the state of society . . . bemoaning the cowardice of the poor, but who at these times . . . were trying to perceive where they had failed, what they had lacked, to be thus vanquished in the race."

It seems to me fruitless to read either of these stories as being very much more symbolic than any piece utilizing language is likely to be. The men who wait outside the lodginghouse are not waiting for a social change, they are waiting to get in out of the cold.[9] If we should even grant that their waiting is symbolic of the need for some kind of social reorganization which would provide for them the basic human needs, then must we not for consistency's sake infer that when the door is opened a social change has occurred? At what point does the door cease to be symbolic and become that which allows access to or egress from the house? One will generally come closer to deriving Crane's meaning when there is much doubt by trusting the realistic rather than the symbolic reading.

"The Dark Brown Dog," another sketch slight in content and significance, has as its theme the cruelty rampant among Bowery inhabitants. The characters are the Johnson family of *Maggie*, Tommie, the child who dies in the earlier story, being the central character.[10] Crane's tone here stands in marked contrast to the tone of "An Experiment in Misery" and "The Men in The Story." The same furious hatred that we saw Crane express toward his characters in *Maggie* he expresses here. Even the baby, Tommie, though becoming sympathetic in the end, is criticized at the beginning of the story for his cruelty toward the little brown puppy that he finds. Acting in a manner not peculiar to the denizens of his Bowery environment, Tommie strikes the dog on the head for no ostensible reason. He continues to beat the dog after discovering that when he does so the dog lies on his back with his paws up as though pleading forgiveness for existing. When the dog begins to follow Tommie home he is beaten with a stick, yet this does not destroy the dog's attachment to the boy. Tommie takes the dog home—beating him all the way—and the father, being in bad temper, allows the dog to stay in order to antagonize the family. Afterwards the boy becomes the friend of the dog, protecting him from the constant, violent abuse of the rest of the family, but himself beating the dog from time to time "although it is not known that he ever had what truly could be called a just cause." The mutual fondness between boy and dog increases as time passes.

The father comes home very drunk one day, hostile and aggressive, angry at the world. He vents his wrath on the "cooking utensils, the furniture, and his wife." Spotting the dog ambling across the floor, he knocks it down with a coffee pot, kicks at it, then finally lays it low with a second blow from the coffee pot. He picks the dog up, swings it about his head, then throws it out the window. It lands five stories below. Later when the family comes looking for Tommie they find him "seated by the body of his dark brown friend."

The cruelty toward the dog exercised by the little boy at the beginning of the story is traced to its roots and shown to stem from the character of the father (whom he imitates in beating the dog), his reaction to his particular familial situation and his Bowery environment. The beginning of the story anticipates its ending, the final cruelty shown to the dog being only a greater degree of that which we see at the opening of the story. Though we feel sympathetic toward Tommie in the end, we are likely to remember that he is potentially (given the continued influence of his environment) as cruel as his father though we should temper this feeling with the knowledge that children from the best families are often cruel enough.

The child who is the central character in "An Ominous Babe" is presumably the same child appearing in "The Dark Brown Dog" and again, presumably, little brother Tommie of *Maggie.* "An Ominous Babe" describes an early experience that the child has with the world outside the Bowery. The babe is "ominous" in the sense that he seems to constitute a threat to the world into which he emerges from his Bowery home. And so he does. "Go 'way, little boy," says the nursemaid of a baby who playfully shakes his rattle at the strange child, "Go 'way. You're all dirty." Eventually he espies a "pretty child in fine clothes playing with a toy." The intruder wants the toy, a bright red fire engine, so he wrenches it away from the other child, then beats a hasty retreat to his Bowery haunt.

Crane passes no negative judgment upon the antisocial act of the Bowery child, choosing instead to ignore the ethical implications of thievery as well as to let lie the social ramifications of the situation beyond simply stating the social contrast involved and implying that the "pretty child" is less experienced in physical combat and thus weaker than the other child. There is a greater degree of sympathy expressed toward the poor Bowery child, but this might be because he is the central character of the story. I would hesitate to speculate on what social implications might be here since underlying the events of the episode is the fact that children are not as responsible as adults are and not having been thoroughly imbued with any ethical or moral sense, are prone to unjust, often cruel acts. Because the central event of the story does not involve adults, it is difficult to view it as different from an act which either child, given the proper circumstances, might have performed.

Another of Crane's short pieces, "The Duel that Was Not Fought," is about Bowery people, but it takes place outside of the Bowery itself. It is singularly of interest because it questions the desirability of valor uninformed by discretion. Crane examines the distinction between courage and foolhardiness, suggesting that courage is not in itself necessarily a valuable attribute.

Patsy Tulligan and two friends, returning to the Bowery from uptown, stop in various saloons on the way back. Patsy, the central character of the story, ". . . was not as wise as seven owls, but his courage could throw a shadow as long as the steeple of a cathedral. There were men on Cherry Street who had whipped him five times, but they all knew that Patsy would be as ready for the sixth time as if nothing had happened." In one of these saloons two well-dressed men smoking cigars, and a "slim little Cuban" are the only other customers. At one point the

Cuban, sitting alone, makes a noise of some kind. The tipsy Patsy makes a loud comment to his friends, using a word "which is no more than passing the time of day down in Cherry Street, but to the Cuban it was a dagger-point." Leaping from his seat, the enraged Cuban confronts Patsy and demands satisfaction. Patsy can only understand that the little man wants to scrap. They argue, but are kept separate by the others. "If you touch me wis your hand, I will keel you," threatens the little Cuban. One of the customers explains to Patsy that the Cuban wishes to duel with swords, and Patsy, who has never in his life had a sword in his hand, says "Well, if he's so dead stuck on fightin' wid swords, I'll fight 'im. Soitenly! I'll fight 'im. . . . Let 'im bring on his swords, an' I'll fight 'im till he's ready to quit." The Cuban, who unconsciously assumes the posture of a fencer, and who has "all the quick, springy movements of a skillful swordsman," would undoubtedly defeat Patsy in a duel, but no such consideration tempers Patsy's anger. After much more argument and jostling, when the tempers of all concerned have risen near to the point of explosion, the bartender rushes out to get a policeman. Upon his return with the policeman, Patsy and the Cuban are preparing to fetch swords from the Cuban's hotel room. The Cuban is arrested because he tells the policeman that the affair is "none of his business." Patsy leaves the saloon having no idea how close he has come to meeting his death.

Patsy, unlike most of Crane's characters who face the possibility of their own deaths, knows not the least fear or doubt of his ability to survive. He is the antithesis of the little man who at some points is petrified by his fear, or of the early Henry Fleming who runs when his life is threatened. Neither response, we should infer, is adequate. The one stems simply from cowardice, the other from foolhardiness. If discretion is not in fact the better part of valor, it at least has some role in distinguishing the hero from the mere fool. Crane does not treat this theme singly again, but we meet another character who develops the attitude exhibited by Patsy. That character, the Swede in

"The Blue Hotel," does not, however, get off so easily.

As honest men must, Crane examined the antitheses of nearly all the major conclusions he came to. For him there were no easy answers, no facile conclusions or solutions to difficult problems. In *The Sullivan County Sketches* Crane examined in detail the possibility and necessity of courageous action. Yet in "The Duel that Was Not Fought" he asks whether courageous action is in itself meaningful, coming to the conclusions that it is not unless tempered with discretion. Feeling that "the root of Bowery life is a sort of cowardice," scorning the characters of *Maggie,* he was able at the same time to muster sufficient sympathetic identification to consider Bowery life from the point of view of Bowery inhabitants. In *Maggie* he worked from the premises of Darwinism (at least as he knew them), seeing his characters as determined by their heredity and environment. *George's Mother* views man as free and responsible for his actions.

We have seen that Crane was not always sure what his attitude toward his materials was. In life, certainly, we cannot always have a consistent, well-defined position on given matters; often such positions tend to falsify or distort reality since all experience cannot be readily defined within strict forms of logic, or in any objective terms. But in art one's point of view, his attitudes toward his materials, must be consistent within the framework of the form itself. That the position which the artist must take might be incompatible with that taken in other works, is of little consequence. He must in each work be consistent in his tone. Crane's inability to maintain always a consistent tone is one of his greatest shortcomings. I suspect that the failure arose from his desire to be true to the "facts" of experience. Sometimes he embodied a theme and its antithesis in the same work rather than considering them as separate and different problems to be considered in separate works. This shortcoming is responsible for the problem of tone in *The Red Badge of Courage.*

4

Crane at War: *The Red Badge*

What is there in *The Red Badge of Courage* which elicits such widespread disagreement concerning what has happened to Henry Fleming by the time the novel closes? There are generally three answers that are given by critics of Crane's best known novel about Henry's position at the end. One answer is that he has achieved nothing, that he is in no better position at the end of the novel than he was at the beginning. Others feel that Henry has achieved moral or spiritual rejuvenation to the extent that he is able at the end of the novel to function more effectually as a human being than he was at the beginning. A third response to the question is one best articulated by Stanley Greenfield in an article titled "The Unmistakable Stephen Crane."

> Man does have will, and he has the ability to reflect, and though these do not guaranty that he can effect his own destiny, they do enable him to become responsible to some degree for the honesty of his personal vision. It is this duality of view, like Chaucer's, that is the secret of the unmistakable Crane's art.[1]

This implies that Henry's success is a "limited success." The assumption of one of these stances underlies practically all criticism of *The Red Badge.* No one of them is adequate.

We cannot easily rest with the conclusion that Henry has achieved nothing by the end of the novel, for there is too much in the novel itself which contradicts such a view. There is for instance the fact of Henry's change from one who flees danger to one who faces it squarely. In spite of the implications that he reverts to primitive sub-human response in acting heroically though in a totally nonconscious fashion, there are evidences of willed acts of heroism. In Chapter XVIII, when Henry and a friend go to seek water, they encounter the general of their division whom they overhear giving orders to a lower-ranking officer. Asked which troops he can spare to serve as cannon fodder in an effort to stop the enemy at a crucial point, the lower-ranking officer replies that he can best spare Henry's division because they are poor fighters. "I don't believe many of your mule drivers will get back," says the general. The conversation leads Henry and his friend to believe that their chances of surviving the coming action are extremely slight, still they return to their group, merely reporting that the regiment is going to charge the enemy, but omitting the information that a death trap awaits them.

> It was an ironical secret. Still, they saw no hesitation in each other's faces, and they nodded a mute and unprotesting assent when a shaggy man near them said in a meek voice, "We'll git swallowed." [2]

Henry's decision to go into that battle indicates a conscious choice to risk the possibility of his own annihilation. Here is the conscious act of heroism.[3]

Other evidence suggesting that Henry undergoes meaningful change is contained in one of the sections expunged by Crane in his manuscript, but reprinted in several recent editions of the novel.[4] Of course it must be considered external evidence. However, it clearly shows Crane's unsuccessful effort to unify the disparate themes of his novel, and it supports the contention that Henry achieves significant growth during the tale because it stands in support of so much that has gone before. The tone of the passage seems straightforward, void of the irony pervading so much of the book.[5]

> And then he regarded it [his guilt about his treatment of the tattered man in Chapters VIII–X] with what he thought to be great calmness. At last he concluded that he

saw in it quaint uses. He exclaimed that its importance in the aftertime would be great to him if it even succeeded in hindering the workings of his egotism. It would make a sobering balance. It would become a good part of him. He would have upon him the consciousness of a great mistake. And he would be taught to deal gently and with care. He would be a man.

It would seem quite odd that Crane would include such a passage in the first place unless something preceding it in the novel had allowed him to consider such sentiments. He would hardly alter the meaning of his novel in one of the final paragraphs; there must have been a number of things which went before, pointing to the possibility of such a conclusion as that quoted above.

In his first engagement after receiving his "red badge" the youth fights courageously, but he seems to have no conscious awareness of what he is about. Thus his courage seems rather meaningless. But later, especially after the color-bearer is killed and Henry takes his place, the youth seems capable of exercising conscious self-control during battle.

The youth, upon hearing the shouts, began to study the distance between him and the enemy. He made vague calculations. He saw that to be firm soldiers they must go forward. It would be death to stay in the present place, and with all the circumstances to go backward would exalt too many others. Their hope was to push the galling foes away from the fence.

Though Henry does not have a gun and must as color-bearer stand exposed to the fire of the enemy, he does not cringe in action, and is more aware of his surroundings during battle than ever before. His reactions here should be compared with those elicited by his exposure to danger in the preceding battle. The reactions exhibited indicate a third level of response to the possibility of his own annihilation. First he runs from danger and possible death. Next he fights, but in an automatic, somnambulistic way. Finally he acts in a highly conscious manner, though in truth there are scattered references to the men as animals and some suggestions that Henry is not entirely aware of his motions. Yet doubtlessly he is a different person from the one who fought in the preceding battles.

Turning once again to the end of the novel, we note another passage, one which Crane left in the novel, which again suggests that Henry had undergone a meaningful change in character.

> And at last his eyes seemed to be opened to some new ways. He found that he could look back upon the brass and bombast of his earlier gospels and see them truly. He was gleeful when he discovered that he now despised them.
>
> With this conviction came a store of assurance. He felt a quiet manhood, nonassertive but of sturdy and strong blood. He knew that he would no more quail before his guides wherever they should point. He had been to touch the great death, and found that, after all, it was but the great death. He was a man.
>
> So it came to pass that as he trudged from the place of blood and wrath his soul changed.

If we consider that the central problem of the tale is defined at the point in the novel at which Henry runs from battle, then considering the material presented above, we can easily substantiate the claim that Henry is no longer a coward. It would appear that he has indeed undergone a change in character sufficient to allow him to respond more adequately to the life situation.

Nevertheless the position supported by evidence like the above, the position declaring that Henry has achieved moral or spiritual rejuvenation, or at least has improved his lot as a human being, is not wholly satisfactory. Legislating against this position is the strong implication, so strong that few critics seem to have missed it, that in the universe of *The Red Badge* man is "nothing but" an animal determined by mechanistic forces over which he exercises no control. There is strong evidence in the novel that Crane intended this inference to be drawn, especially in Chapter XVII where Henry is about to engage in the first battle after having received his "red badge." This is the reading that many who have desired to place Crane firmly in the naturalistic camp have made. Certainly in such a world Henry could not have transcended the limits imposed by nature through conscious effort of will.

Passages deleted by Crane at the end of the manuscript are again relevant here. And again it is of significance that he saw fit to expunge them. They obviously run counter to an effect he wishes to produce *after the fact* of the writing of the novel.

> Fate had in truth been kind to him; she had stabbed him with benign purpose and diligently cudgelled him for his own sake. In his rebellion, he had been very portentous, no doubt, and sincere, and anxious for humanity, but now that he stood safe, with no lack of blood, it was suddenly clear to him that he had been wrong not to kiss the knife and bow to the cudgel. He had foolishly squirmed.

> With his new eyes, he could see that the secret and open blows which were being dealt about the world with such heavenly lavishness were in truth blessings. It was a deity laying about him with the bludgeon of correction.

The irony in these passages seems unmistakable to me. The implication of them is one of Crane's recurring themes, that man is an alien in an alien universe, and all the works of his days and hands come to naught. Thus when Henry felt that "he was tiny but not inconsequent to the sun," that "in the spacewide whirl of events no grain like him would be lost," he is deluding himself in the same manner he so often deluded himself before. Only a fool would have "turned now with a lover's thirst to images of tranquil skies, fresh meadows, cool brooks—an existence of soft and eternal peace," as Henry does in the next to last sentence of the novel as Crane published it. No one leads or ever has led "an existence of soft and eternal peace."

Equally devastating to the position defending meaningful growth on the part of the hero is the last line of the novel, "Over the river a golden ray of sun came through the hosts of leaden rain clouds." If Henry has learned anything, he should know that he cannot trust any such sign from nature, that though nature might be beautiful and appealing it has no messages for men, especially messages presaging good fortune. Certainly after having been tricked so many times by nature, he would not be taken in again if he had the least bit of sense. Even if the last sentence should represent the point of view of the author rather than Henry, it yet raises problems of consistency. It has been Crane's view all along that nature is alien to man. Having read the novel up to the last page, no sensitive reader is going to accept signs from nature as meaningful.

In one sentence near the end of the novel, a sentence Crane left in his final version, he again implies that Henry's acts through the course of the novel are insignificant because Henry's perspective is just as distorted as it has been earlier in the story. "He saw that he was good." Does this short sentence call anything to mind, its structure, its diction, its rhythm? Recall Genesis 1: 10, "And God called the dry land Earth; and the gathering together of the waters called the Seas: and *God saw that it was good.*" Henry's pride at the end of the novel is so overweening, his view of himself so distorted, that he equates himself with God. Evidence of this kind is ignored by those who wish to show that Henry has achieved moral or spiritual rejuvenation or that he has at least by the end of the novel become better able to function in the world.

The irony of *The Red Badge* serves Crane's intentions well only if he intended to convince the reader that Henry's seemingly heroic gestures were futile, and it of course seems doubtful that this is an adequate description of his total intention. As in *Maggie*, the irony creates an unbreachable gap between author and character and between reader and character. As late in the action as Chapter XV Crane subjects Henry to the most devastating and sustained irony appearing anywhere in the book. In this section occurs the episode in which Henry's friend Wilson asks him to return a packet of letters which he, fearing that he would not survive the battle during which Henry runs, had entrusted to him. Henry, forgetting that he ran from the battle while Wilson stayed and fought, assumes an extremely patronizing air, feeling derision for one who had been foolish enough to reveal weakness. He considers the letters a weapon "with which he could prostrate his comrade at the first signs of a cross examination." Only a person who was not very worthwhile could take such an attitude. Henry also feels superior to other soldiers who like him had run from battle. If Crane intends to show by the end of the novel that Henry performs meaningful, heroic action, then it will be necessary to repair the disruption of affection between reader and character. Otherwise, we are likely to believe that one capable of deluding himself to such an extreme degree is not likely to change his character over the short period of time between this chapter and the end of the book.

It is relevant that Crane removed much of the irony from this chapter before publishing it, though a great deal (the quotation below for example) yet remains. Had he removed all the irony, nothing would have remained of the chapter. Were we to compare the sections expunged here with those taken out near the end of the book, we would note a great similarity, especially if we have in mind Henry's notions of his own role in the cosmic scheme, and more particularly of his relation to nature.

> He returned to his old belief in the ultimate, astounding success of life. He as usual, did not trouble about processes. It was ordained, because he was a fine creation. He saw plainly that he was the chosen of some gods. By fearful and wonderful roads he was to be led to a crown. He was, of course, satisfied that he deserved it.

But the greater support for the case against the meaningfulness of Henry's actions lies in comparing what Crane left in Chapter XV with what Crane left in the final chapter.

The foregoing discussion should suggest something of the difficulty involved in attempting to reconcile the antithetical themes of *The Red Badge* by reference to any kind of duality of vision. We would be closer to the truth of the matter by recognizing that Crane has written two books in *The Red Badge,* each of which has its own theme, and the two themes are mutually exclusive. The novel does not "show up the nature and value of courage." On the contrary it asks whether courage is meaningful in the world, then it asks what is the nature of the world. Is nature, is the cosmic structure of the world, meaningful? If so, then a heroic ideal is possible; if not, then no action that man could perform could be significant beyond his own delusions. Because Crane could not answer the latter question, he could not answer the former. Hence, a rupture in the author's view of his materials; hence a rupture in the final meaning of the book. Had the novel manifested a duality of view, then we might assume that the author believed simultaneously in the possibility of a meaningful courage and in a world in which courage was meaningless because all actions and attitudes of men were ultimately meaningless. There is a difference between believing both of these equally and seeing the two as alternatives, but trusting the validity of neither.[6]

The two major strains running through *The Red Badge* we have seen developed in Crane's earlier fiction. The one strain, which sees the value and necessity of heroism, of ability to act freely, unconstrained by the limitations imposed upon action by fear, was explored in *The Sullivan County Sketches. George's Mother* presented the same problem, but in a different way. That novel dealt with the limitations on free action resulting from the imposition of external authority by the parent, a situation which thwarts the development of the individual and requires exertion of will to overcome. *Maggie,* the most naturalistic piece of Crane's writing so far discussed, embodies the other strain. In this novel man is depicted as completely determined by his heredity and his environment, powerless to perform any action willfully, incapable of contributing to the development of his own character. In a certain sense *The Red Badge* is a culmination, a record of the direction of Crane's thought up to about 1895, its date of publication.

Never again was Crane to write from the assumption that man had no responsibility in the determination of his own fate. From this point in his fiction man is often the victim of circumstances, but never completely out of control of his fate.

It is fortunate that we have the manuscript of *The Red Badge of Courage*, for it solves the problem of Crane's intention in the novel. The deletions in the manuscript point toward one conclusion: Crane saw that his novel lacked unity; consequently he attempted to supply unity by striking out those passages antithetical to the image of the novel which he formed *after the fact of having written the novel*.[7] For this reason we are able to distinguish between the novel Crane actually wrote and the one he *wished* to present to the public. Clearly they are not the same.

It is significant that Crane was not able to disguise the disparity existing between the two themes of the novel by striking out certain passages. Had he been able to do this, then the controversy surrounding the meaning of the novel would not exist. But deleting entirely the evidence suggesting that Henry Fleming has accomplished nothing meaningful by the end of the novel would have destroyed the novel and required a complete rewriting job. Again, this points to the fact that the very conception of the novel led to the birth of twins, fraternal, not identical.

We will never know exactly why Crane chose to make public the one novel but not the other. There are a multitude of possibilities, but all of them are purely speculative. In any case it is clear that only one of these novels was sufficiently developed to allow publication without complete rewriting. This suggests the direction of Crane's emphasis. It suggests that of the two novels one was foremost in his mind, and that *one* is the traditional story of the hero, beset by great odds, who through fortitude and endurance is able to achieve his ends. Let us examine that novel.

Henry Fleming is a composite of the little man of *The Sullivan County Sketches* and George of *George's Mother*. Like these two, he has as his central problem the strengthening of his consciousness to the extent that he will be able to act freely, unconstrained by fear, in the world. But, unlike his predecessors, Henry Fleming is eventually strong enough to face the possibility of the actual extinction of his own ego. The fears which the little man faces are shown time and time again to be groundless, the product of an overactive imagination; those of George are real enough, perhaps even equal to the fears one might have in the face of physical death, but the outcome of his conflict with Mrs. Kelcey would hardly result in his physical destruction. Henry, at the beginning of the novel, is one step ahead of George by virtue of having repudiated the claims of his parent by joining the army against her will, thus separating himself from the costly support of pre-existent authority.

But his separation is not an easy one, nor is it immediately permanent. We learn in the first chapter that Henry has a firm attachment to his mother. We infer this from the amount of time it takes him to decide he is going to join the army in spite of her wishes. He does finally make "firm rebellion" against her, but when the time comes to depart, his excitement and expectancy only *almost* defeat "the glow of regret for the home bonds." Taking leave of his mother, Henry does not feel the elation he must have expected to feel from having fulfilled a long-standing wish. Seeing "her brown face, upraised, stained with tears, and her spare form quivering," he bows his head, "feeling suddenly ashamed of his purposes." Several times during the course of the novel's action, he indicates that his break with his former identity is not complete, wishing he were back at home, absolved of the responsibility of free action, and safe from the threat of extinction by the opposing army. His attempt to bury himself during the forest chapel scene suggests this same hesitancy and doubt about his own ability to survive alone in the world.

It would be quite unusual for one Henry's age to know the nature of his psychic situation as thoroughly as he does at the beginning of the novel. But because of the youth's particular situation, being a soldier in wartime, he is immediately in a position demanding the testing of his strengths and limitations. In ordinary life, one would probably not find himself faced with the immediate and acute necessity of coming to grips with the problem of identity. But this is one way in which the war background of the novel serves Crane's ends well. Here it allows him to telescope a phenomenon which might have taken months or years, suggesting the limited sense in which this is a war novel.

Henry knows that his next move after leaving home must be toward discovering who and what he is, and eventually toward discovering his relation to the universe at large; later in the novel he becomes aware that the two questions are intimately linked. Chapter I reveals his concern with discovering a new definition of himself through knowledge of his strengths and limitations. "He felt that in this crisis his laws of life were useless. . . . He was an unknown quantity. . . . He must accumulate information of himself." Like a child lost, he seeks to learn how others feel about the impending trial, asking one and then the other in a manner calculated to mask his own trepidation. Eventually, he discovers that he is alone, "separated from the others," as of course each person who attempts to know himself is alone. Such journeys within allow for no companions. At first Henry cannot bear his isolation from his fellows; he is not yet sufficiently strong. On an evening shortly after the time of the actual beginning of the novel, Henry withdraws from his companions—companions with whom he feels little accord—wandering into the evening gloom.

> He lay down in the grass. The blades pressed tenderly against his cheek. The moon had been lighted and was hung in a treetop. The liquid stillness of the night enveloping him made him feel vast pity for himself. There was a caress in the soft winds; and the whole mood of the darkness, he thought, was one of sympathy for himself in his distress.

This is one of the key passages in the novel. For the first time Henry feels that nature is actively sympathetic toward him and toward his particular ends. So powerfully does he feel nature's compassion for him that he imagines she "envelopes" him, protecting him from any antagonistic forces without. He imagines himself momentarily in a womb where he is protected, nourished, sustained, where there are no problems to be met, no dragons to be encountered. The grass lovingly presses "tenderly against his cheek" and the soft wind caresses him. This very same sensation, this very escape, is what Henry seeks when he burrows into the woods in the forest chapel scene later on in Chapter VII.

The paragraph immediately following this gives us a clue to the interpretation of the preceding passage as well as of the forest chapel scene. What follows but the youth's firm wish that he were home again, "He wished, without reserve, that he was at home again making the endless rounds from the house to the barn, from the barn to the fields, from the fields to the barn, from the barn to the house." He associates a constellation of ideas that he sees in nature with a constellation of ideas associated with home. In wishing to return home, it is not simply that Henry wishes to return to the womb; rather he wants to return to his situation prior to joining the army. He wants to return to his mother who defined for him who and what he was, who differentiated right from wrong, who provided for him a knowledge of the way things are. This is one of the instances in which Henry's feeble consciousness wishes to regress to a former state. Eventually he will become strong enough to forego indulgence in such meaningless fantasies, but not before a number of womb-shattering experiences. Meanwhile he wishes from time to time that he didn't have such monstrously large problems to solve.

The first four chapters describe Henry's attempts to prepare himself psychologically for the conflict occurring in Chapter V. In spite of the fact that Henry decides as early as Chapter II that intellectualization will not lead him to a conclusion about what his reactions in battle will be, that the only way of knowing his responses is to "have blaze, blood, and danger, even as a chemist requires this, that and the other," he continues to speculate up to the time of the battle about how he will react. We can in part trace Henry's difficulties to an overactive imagination, to his too great willingness to decide conclusively the outcome of his encounter with opposition, but his imagination accounts only in part for his difficulties.

During his first battle (Chapter V) the youth does indeed suspend the functioning of his imagination; he suspends indeed nearly all conscious functioning, all but a dim animal awareness that his situation is uncomfortable and that his fighting has something to do with alleviating the discomfort of the situation: "He developed the acute exasperation of a pestered animal, a well-meaning cow worried by dogs." He also has dim awareness of a "subtle battle brotherhood. . . . a mysterious fraternity born of the smoke and danger of death." But throughout the scene, the youth is described as being in a "battle sleep." He fights "for respite of his senses, for air, as a babe being smothered attacks the deadly blankets." At the beginning of Chapter VI, "the youth awakened slowly. He came gradually back to a position from which he could regard himself." Here the youth has been able to disregard the question of his survival, to suspend the activity of his imagination and thus function in what is to him a desirable fashion.

But to Crane this is not enough. Henry's ability to suspend the functioning of his imagination during the first encounter by no means insures his having achieved courage. At the next encounter Henry becomes acutely conscious of himself and his situation, tumbling once more into the trap formed by his imagination. His body begins to fail him. "His neck was quivering with nervous weakness and the muscles of his arms felt numb and bloodless. . . . There was a great uncertainty about his knee joints." Then he begins to think about the enemy and about the power of the enemy, exaggerating "the endurance, the skill, and the valor of those who were coming." Here the youth's own feelings, coupled with his observance of those of his fellow soldiers who are likewise victims of their imaginations, result in his complete loss of control of himself and his situation. Up to this point Crane has apparently shown that cowardice results from the inability to suspend the functioning of the imagination. "Directly he began to speed toward the rear in great leaps. . . . On his face was all the horror of those things which he imagined."

After his flight his fortunes are and continue to be at lowest ebb from Chapter VII to Chapter XIII in which he returns to his regiment. The experiences he undergoes during the central portion of the book allow him to act as he does during the final battles. This withdrawal from the scene of battle, from a situation in which his own extinction is imminent, seems necessary if he is to recoup his internal forces sufficiently to allow him once again to expose himself to the possibility of death.

Significantly enough, the first act after his flight is to retreat into the forest, "as if resolved to bury himself."[8] Previously Henry has wished to bury himself, in the third chapter, where, feeling unjustly accused of lagging behind his group, he thinks "he must look to the grave for comprehension." His journey into the forest is an enactment of the fantasy he has in chapter two where he imagines that he is enveloped by "the liquid stillness of the night." Here in Chapter VII he seeks to bring the feelings generated by his fantasy into conjunction with the real world. In the past he has only *wished* to return home, to his mother, to the safety of his rural past. In this case he acts out his deepest desires to retreat from the world to the safety of an existence where he will be free from fear, where he will be protected and sustained, out of sight of the world and sheltered from its harsh judgments, where, in short, he will be required to exercise none of the functions of consciousness. He goes far into the wood, "seeking dark and intricate places." If he goes far enough, he believes he will escape extinction, putting behind him, as he does, "the rumble of death."

Henry feels closer to nature here than anywhere else in

the novel. He has the impression that nature not only will comfort and succor him in the time of need, but that she will actively reveal to him ethical truth. The squirrel in the forest, running when Henry throws a pine cone at it, justifies to Henry his own conduct in running when threatened by danger. "Nature had given him a sign." But Henry fails to interpret properly the scene he sees immediately afterward. A small animal dives into a pool of water and emerges with a fish. This should have told Henry that his feeling that there was only benevolence in nature needed correction. Had he seen the significance of this event, he would have been closer to discovering his true relationship to nature. But obviously Henry is seeing only what he wants to see, creating the external world again, not as it is, but as he would have it be.

Deeper and deeper Henry burrows into the forest, "going from obscurity to promises of greater obscurity." Eventually he reaches a seemingly enclosed area, a place where he might hope to be enveloped in "liquid stillness." Pushing aside the green doors, he steps into a region where pine needles form a gentle, brown carpet and where a religious half-light overspreads the whole. If he is to find peace anywhere in nature it should be here; here should be the place where nature will take him to her bosom if she ever will. But such is not Henry's fate, nor is such the character of nature. In the very heart of the forest Henry finds not safety, escape from death, comfort, succor, peace, but death, death at the very center of nature. It would be difficult to imagine a more horrible spectacle than that which the youth sees. The descriptive details indicate a most appalling, terrifying scene. It is fitting that Henry should be met with such a sight, since he must be disabused of his faith in a sympathetic nature.

Henry meets death in the womb. Having gone as far as he has in his psychic development, he cannot turn back. He is no longer free to escape from the world without a kind of death occurring, the death of that facet of his character which finds itself dissatisfied with his failure to meet the world squarely, to deal with the life situation in order to exercise some control over it. Death is in the womb as well as without. There is no choice but to come to terms with the possibility of his own destruction.

Here Henry is reborn, at least in this novel of the two Crane combined in *The Red Badge*. He should learn here that nature does not work in accord with man's needs and desires, that, in fact, nature in its indifference is more likely to seem hostile than helpful. And so it is, insofar as Henry's needs are concerned. Nature seems to attempt to hold him, in feminine, maternal fashion, because in undergoing the development of consciousness, he intends to separate himself from nature, to replace the instinctive imperative to action with consciously controlled action, with self-imposed imperatives. As an animal he participates in nature, is controlled by nature, is subject to subrational responses. "The branches, pushing against him, threatened to throw him over upon [the body]," thereby threatening to bring about the death of consciousness, which by its very essence is antagonistic to nature. "His unguided [not consciously directed] feet, too, caught aggravatingly in brambles; and with it all he received a subtle suggestion to touch the corpse." But Henry's feeble consciousness is yet strong enough to oppose successfully the desire to accept gladly the demise of his will to separate himself from nature. "As he thought of his hand upon the corpse he shuddered profoundly." He is able to flee: "At last he burst the bonds [umbilical I would say] which had fastened him to the spot and fled, *unheeding* the underbrush." (My emphasis) Because he is able to flee he should have been reborn, as indeed he is in Crane's central novel.

Since we are dealing with two novels in *The Red Badge*, each of which has a different theme, it is impossible to say in a simple sentence what the final outcome of this scene is. The primary novel, the one in which Crane seems to have had most faith and the one which he tried to create by deleting the antithetical elements, tells us that Henry was reborn as a result of his forest-chapel experience; that he learns that nature is not the least sympathetic toward man's hopes and aspirations. After his experience in the forest the youth is in a position to achieve the goal of his quest by having in large measure severed his ties with nature, becoming dependent upon his own resources. Had this scene not occurred, Henry would not have been able to return to his regiment, and subsequently be capable of heroic action. His experience is a learning experience.

I have spoken of nature here as being an active participant in the action of this scene. It remains to be said in what sense this is so. On first glance it might seem that Crane, in attributing purposeful activity to nature here as elsewhere in the novel, had involved himself in the pathetic fallacy. But how inconsistent this would be. So often we see nature apparently going about her business, completely uninvolved in the affairs of men going on around her. Just as nature lacks the consciousness to support men in the achievement of their ends, so she lacks the consciousness implied in thwarting goals. When after the forest-chapel scene Henry is finding his way out of the forest, it seems to him that nature actively opposes him. "Sometimes the brambles formed chains and tried to hold him back." Henry, not Crane, views nature as actively hostile. The youth projects onto nature his own feelings about his place in nature, in the universal scheme of things. That particular facet of his psyche which sees the brambles forming chains to hold him back is an anti-self, a force directing him toward the submergence of his developing consciousness in the very nature from whence it arises. This anti-conscious pull is a negative force comprising all those desires which the youth has to return to the comfort and security of home, of his mother, to evade the expenditure of energy necessary in confronting the world and its ever-threatening destructive potential. The conflict which is *apparently* between the youth and a hostile nature is in fact the conflict existing within the youth. Consequently we should be able to guage the youth's progress toward the development of consciousness by noting his responses to nature. When he is furthest away from achieving his goals he should identify himself with nature, seeing himself involved in her processes to the extent that

conscious activity is not a value to him. We should expect
that when he is strong enough to face the possibility of his
own destruction, he will no longer identify with nature,
will not see nature as an antagonistic force because he will
have freed himself from nature's domain. Such is indeed
the case. After Chapter XV, the chapter contributing
most to the thesis that Henry's struggle has been a completely meaningless one, the youth no longer sees nature
as being kind and benevolent until the very last chapter
where confusion once again rears its ignoble head, and the
two novels which Crane wrote again battle for supremacy.
Once he has broken the ties that bind, he need no longer
fear—he need no longer see in nature an adversary. Thus
nature need not seem an active participant in the events of
the novel after the resolution of the conflict within Henry.

From Chapter VIII to the end of Chapter XII Henry
assimilates the knowledge gained from his experience in
the forest chapel. His movement from Chapter VI to the
end of Chapter VII (the forest-chapel scene) has been
away from battle. A reversal occurs in the latter chapter,
sending Henry back toward his regiment. But before he
returns, he undergoes several experiences which reinforce
the implications to him of his experience in the wilderness. All that he experiences during this time tells him
that he is not nature's darling, that nature does not involve herself in the affairs of men.

As he "obstinately" proceeds from the heart of the
forest "on his forward way," he comes upon a battlefield
deserted except for corpses lying amidst clothes and guns.
He is apprehensive, yet he experiences nothing of the horror called forth by his previous confrontation with the
dead. Here he notices that nature has had nothing to do
with the facts before him. She has neither cared nor not
cared. "A hot sun had [?] blazed upon the spot."

Throughout the succeeding chapters the youth feels
increasingly guilty for having run away from battle. The
tattered man whom he meets in the procession of
wounded soldiers moving toward the rear seems to objec-
tify the feelings of guilt stirring within the youth. Dogging

his steps like some specter from his conscience, the tat-tered man, "fouled with dust, blood and powder," is a constant reminder to Henry of his cowardice. "Where yeh hit, ol' boy?" he asks.

Meeting Jim Conklin, the youth feels even more guilt-ridden than before, for Jim Conklin is someone he knows. This encounter is important in the experience of Henry Fleming, but it is important only in light of what has pre-ceded. Death becomes more meaningful to Henry than it has ever been before as he watches his comrade Jim Conk-lin in the throes of death. Prior to this episode, he had been awed more by the idea of death than by death itself. Here death becomes an actuality. "The youth had watched, spellbound, this ceremony at the place of meeting. His face had been twisted into an expression of every agony he had imagined for his friend." And finally, "The red sun was pasted in the sky like a wafer." The lesson that the youth learned earlier in the forest chapel is repeated: neither caring nor not caring, nature moves on her way, oblivious to the fortunes of men.

No longer does the youth have the desire to seek "dark and intricate places," but instead "A certain mothlike quality keeps him in the vicinity of the battle." The fact of his lingering about the battle suggests that his receiving his "red badge" is not so much a fortuitous circumstance as has been heretofore supposed by practically everyone who has written about the novel. At the time he receives it, he is in the midst of an army in wild retreat. Seeing the routed army charging "down upon him like terrified buffaloes," Henry forgets "his mental pamphlets on the philosophy of the retreated and rules for the guidance of the damned." And in a line deleted by Crane from the published text, "He lost concern for himself." In spite of the obvious fact that this army is about "to be swallowed" by "war, the blood-swollen god," Henry stands his ground, not wishing to run, but "to make a rallying speech, to sing to a battle hymn." Because he does not involve himself in the hysteria of the crowd, he is rewarded with "a little red badge of courage."

Afterward, the youth shows himself worthy of his reward, for he shows an increasing ability to perform consciously in opposition to his animal self, which urges him to follow the dictates of his body. The inclination of his body is to do nothing, to remain motionless, to sink down overcome by the mindless forces of nature. But instead "He fought an intense battle with his body." From its beginning this scene indicates that Henry is finally beginning to achieve the necessary control of his actions.

But his development from that central episode occurring during the forest-chapel scene is not linear in its movement. He regresses from that initial level of strength and self-confidence which allowed him to leave home to join the army; he regresses from the level of conscious development he has attained through introspection following his act of cowardice. Immediately after his wound he becomes frightened, doubting the whole value of his progression toward the achievement of individuality. As might be expected, he turns his thoughts toward home, yearning for the comfort, security, protection and nourishment afforded by a situation in which he has neither the need nor the desire to be an independent individual, responsible for his own well-being in the world, and subject to the consequences of his own judgments.

> He bethought him of certain meals his mother had cooked at home. . . . The pine walls of the kitchen were glowing in the warm light from the stove. Too, he remembered how he and his companions used to go from the schoolhouse to the bank of a shaded pool. . . . He felt the swash of the fragrant water upon his body. The leaves of the overhanging maple rustled with melody in the wind of youthful summer.

The constellation of ideas associated by Henry with the undeveloped consciousness, with the state of being antithetical to that which he feels the driving need to attain, occurs here explicitly: home, mother, warmth, nourishment. Further, nonconsciousness is again revealed to be a state characteristic of the realm of nature. In being in the water he is immersed in nature, confined comfortably by the water below and by the overhanging maple above. This passage sheds light on the forest-chapel scene, revealing the relationship which Henry feels between nature and his state prior to joining the army. It shows that when Henry retreats from the apparent security of nature, he is retreating not only from nature, but from a complex set of earlier ties.

Significantly enough, after Henry has thought about his previous life he is overcome "by a dragging weariness." No longer does he walk "tall soldier fashion" as he had after receiving his wound, but now his head hangs forward, his shoulders are stooped, his feet shuffle along the ground. Like the song of the sirens, the call of nature attempts to lull him back into nature's domains.

Here when the youth's fortunes are again at low ebb, a series of events is initiated which in the context of the novel seems quite bizarre. Out of nowhere a stranger appears, "the man of the cheery voice." [9] He takes Henry firmly by the arm, at a time when he is in great need of support, saying, "I'm going your way," though, there is nothing in the context to suggest that he has any natural means of knowing which way the youth is going. The man of the cheery voice asks the youth which regiment he belongs to, and, being told, he undertakes to lead Henry there. "They're 'way over in the center," he says. "It'll be a miracle if we find our reg'ments t'-night," he says during the course of his continual chatter, Henry remaining quiet all the while. And it seems that this man does perform a miracle. He seems a wizard in his resourcefulness, in his ability to find his way in the darkness of night and the confusion of war. Leading the youth "without mistakes," the stranger eventually points out a campfire in the distance, directing the youth toward it. He clasps Henry's hand, wishes him good luck, and strides away, whistling audaciously and cheerfully. Suddenly Henry becomes aware "that he had not once seen his face."

This scene contains the most explicit reference to the fairy-tale or mythical motif underlying the events of *The*

Red Badge. We saw this same motif woven within *The Sullivan County Sketches.* Throughout the first half of the novel the youth sees the opposing army as a dragon seeking to devour him. This construct which he puts onto the events occurring during his second battle is largely responsible for his flight. Here he attributes powers to the enemy much greater than those they possess, seeing their approach as "an onslaught of redoubtable dragons."

As long as Henry fears being eaten by the dragon, rather than hoping to slay it by means of his own strength, in actuality, rather than facing it and allowing for the possibility of his own destruction, he will be a victim of his own fear, unable to function autonomously in the world. But just as Henry seems about to relinquish his claims to higher consciousness, soon after he has engaged in the wish-fulfilling fantasy which transports him imaginatively back to the comfort and security of home, the man of the cheery voice appears.

This mysterious man is comparable to the figure who in myth and legend gives aid to the hero faced with tasks beyond the limits of his capacities. Such figures are Ariadne, who tells Theseus how to find his way out of the labyrinth; Athene, who stands by Ulysses, aiding him throughout the course of his adventures in *The Odyssey;* the Cumaean Sibyl, whose directions allow Aeneas to enter and return from the underworld; Virgil, who leads Dante through the underworld; and the innumerable figures in fairy tales who tell the hero how he must go about achieving his task, warn him against dangers which he must overcome or encourage him toward his goal.[10] At the time Henry meets the man of the cheery voice the youth is not heading toward any specific place, nor has he even made the decision to return to his regiment. The strange man leads Henry back, which suggests that he has a supernatural awareness of Henry's deepest needs at the particular time when he meets him. Supporting the youth both physically and morally, presenting to him an example of strength and resourcefulness, the man of the cheery voice, not Henry himself, puts the youth in the position of being able once again to encounter the forces which threaten him but with which he must come to terms.

This man, whose abilities seem to Henry to be magical, presents a striking contrast to other figures in the book because he seems to be on a different plane of existence. It is odd to meet a wizard in an apparently realistic context. But the man of the cheery voice is not such an enigma after all if we take into account the matter of point of view here, nor is it strange that a fairy-tale motif should underlie the plot of a novel which means to be primarily realistic. Since the point of view of *The Red Badge* is the third person restricted view, we are seeing events as they are interpreted by Henry, suggesting that what Henry sees or feels and what Crane sees and feels are not necessarily the same things. In the episode involving the man of the cheery voice, however, the tone indicates that Henry's interpretation of the events occurring there is not at odds with Crane's attitudes. There is none of that irony that occurs when Henry distorts his view of himself or his surroundings. We might conclude thereby that Crane feels that Henry's view of his total situation as being analogous to the situation of the hero of myth and legend is a not inadequate means of description. The point of view allows this magical man to appear without imposing on Crane the necessity of committing himself by implication to the proposition that the world is so constituted that the supernatural does in fact intervene in the affairs of men.

Chapters XIII to XVI inclusive involve Henry's preparation for his renewed encounter with the enemy force. These chapters allow a reader to believe in the possibility of a change in Henry sufficiently great to allow him to perform as he does in the next battle. In Chapter XIII the youth discovers that he is not scorned by his companions, that they in fact believe he has participated bravely in the preceding battle. Chapter XIV reveals the youth's awareness of the great change which has taken place in the loud soldier, suggesting to him by comparison (Henry often evaluates himself in terms of others) that he too could acquire the self-reliance, the inward confidence radiating from the other. Chapter XV, the section contributing most to the book's failure to maintain adequate unity of tone and theme, shows Henry become ridiculously over-confident of his own strengths and perceptions. Neverthe-less it would seem that his distorted self-image contributes to his eventual ability to perform well on the battlefield in much the same way that Christy Mahon's fantasy about killing his "da" determines what Christy becomes through the course of the action of Synge's *Playboy of the West-ern World.* Henry distorts reality in seeing himself as superior to his fellows, in achieving "a mighty scorn for such a snivelling race," yet he in fact grows into the image of himself projected in this chapter. His feeling that "he had been out among the dragons . . . and assured himself that they were not so hideous as he had imagined," seems ludicrous here, but when he later makes the statement it seems a natural outgrowth of the experiences he has un-dergone (unless of course the outcome is read as ironic). Chapter XVI corrects the impression of the preceding chapter by showing us Henry's wariness prior to the com-ing encounter. No longer is he the proud, arrogant swag-gerer we saw a short time before. At the same time, his imagination seems in good control; he is living in the moment without thinking about his own fate.

As I suggested earlier, the ability to suspend the func-tioning of the imagination, to live only in the present moment, is for Crane not enough. The last three encoun-ters of the novel (there are five in all) show Henry grow-ing beyond that requirement. In the very first battle in the book the youth is able to accomplish this function. Still the question remains, why continue the novel beyond the point at which he fights fiercely, where he feels "the supreme trial had been passed. The red, formidable dif-ficulties of war had been vanquished"? That is, why has Henry not achieved his goal at the end of the first encoun-ter? There should be a reason above and beyond the fact that Crane simply wanted to continue the action. In fact there are at least two such reasons. One is that Henry has not really acted courageously, for to Crane courageous action must be conscious action. In this first encounter Henry has no consciousness of what he is about. He works at his weapon "like an automatic affair"; he tries "to rally his faltering intellect so that he might recollect the moment when he had loaded, but he could not"; he is in a "battle sleep" which after the battle he awakes from. It is during this battle and the next that Henry and his comrades are most frequently compared to animals.

The other reason Crane continued the plot beyond Henry's first battle is that Henry's ability to remain in the battle lines at that point is entirely dependent upon his identification with something larger than himself, "a regiment, an army, a cause, or a country." He does not feel at that time the personal involvement necessary for the achievement of his own individuality. He is "welded into a common personality which is dominated by a single desire." The struggle which he is really engaged in, the struggle within himself, must be dealt with alone if he is to resolve it meaningfully.[11] Since "for some moments he could not flee any more than a little finger can commit revolution from a hand," he is not involved in an act of personal courage. Consequently, because he has not vanquished the dragons threatening the extinction of his own being, it is not surprising that the action continues, and it is not less surprising that he runs away during the next battle.

In general Henry's failure to achieve personal courage during the first battle accounts for his cowardice in the second but there are more specific reasons. First the emotions eliciting his feeling about the "subtle brotherhood of battle" betray him in the second battle. When Henry's companions see that they are about to be attacked a second time, they sorrowfully doubt their ability to withstand the assault. They groan, the luster fades from their eyes, their faces reveal profound dejection. Because Henry has been unable to detach himself from the group, he is as much affected by their moods and reactions in one situation as in another. When the men are unwilling to face a formidable foe, then Henry is likewise unwilling, for his apparent courage has been too greatly a result of the support given him by his comrades. If they fight, he fights. If they run (or at least seem to him to run), he runs. The expressions of loss of confidence uttered by his companions recur to him, then he begins to exaggerate the "endurance, skill and the valor of those who were coming." Had Henry possessed personal assurance, had he developed a sufficient degree of self-dependence, he would not have been so greatly influenced by the actions and attitudes of those around him.

Throughout the earlier part of the book, Henry compares himself with others, indicating unawareness of his own identity, of how he should think and act. His great willingness to accept what he believes to be a sign from nature (when he throws the pine cone at the squirrel) is a manifestation of the same lack of selfhood. Seeing a few of his companions throw down their arms and run, Henry cannot but do likewise, again looking outward rather than inward for guidance and assurance about how he should feel and act.

Henry's third encounter is fought much like the first, though close observation of what goes on there will reveal that since his flight from the preceding battle, Henry has made some progress toward his ultimate goal. During the first engagement Henry "developed the acute exasperation of a pestered animal, a well-meaning cow worried by dogs." In this battle his feelings are very much the same: "He was not going to be badgered all of his life, like a kitten chased by boys, he said. It was not well to drive men into final corners; at those moments they could all develop teeth and claws." Again his actions are described by means of metaphors relating to animals. "He crouched behind a little tree, with his eyes burning hatefully, and his teeth set in a cur-like snarl." And again, "When the enemy seemed falling back before him and his fellows, he went instantly forward, like a dog . . ." After the encounter, the youth reflecting on what has gone before, feels "that he had been a barbarian, a beast." The implication of such descriptions is that still the youth is acting instinctively, not exhibiting true courage.

At the same time it is made clear that as in the first encounter the youth is in a "battle sleep." The beginning of the encounter sees him quite unconscious of himself and his surroundings "The youth was not conscious that he was erect upon his feet. He did not know the direction of the ground." When a lull occurs in the firing, Henry is not aware of it until a companion calls out, awakening him. "He had slept," Henry says in retrospect, "and awakening, found himself a knight." Unlike the second battle where he fears the possibility of dying, the third battle finds Henry only once, and only fleetingly aware of what might happen to him during the course of the fight. Yet he has further to go in achieving what Crane believes to be heroism. He must separate himself from nature even further by performing the conscious act of heroism. This occurs in the next battle, the fourth.[12]

Henry enters the fourth engagement with the firm realization that his chances for survival are slight. He has overheard the general of his division tell one of his regimental officers that Henry's regiment will probably be destroyed. Still Henry goes into battle having no conscious concern about his own personal fate. For the first time in the novel, he is able, in full awareness, to face the probability of his own destruction.

During this encounter the youth is not unconscious of his surroundings as he has always been heretofore. No longer is it necessary that he go into a battle sleep; on the contrary his awareness seems even heightened: "It seemed to the youth that he saw everything. Each blade of the green grass was bold and clear. He thought that he was aware of every change in the thin transparent vapor that floated idly in sheets."

When the color sergeant of his regiment is killed, Henry gains possession of the flag. As color-bearer he appears to act even more heroically since he must stand in the fore, unarmed, and an obvious target for opposing riflemen. His new role also finds him being a leader rather than a follower, a manipulator rather than manipulated. Contrary to his way in the second battle and elsewhere in the book, he does not now take his cues for thought and action from those around him. When his companions lag, when they turn from the battle fearful and dismayed, when others hide, "curled into depressions," Henry exhorts them to fight, no longer feeling the fear which had so controlled his actions before. All through the battle he is acutely aware of his surroundings, his new inner strength being sufficiently great to allow him to hold his ground in spite of impending death.

The fifth and final encounter confirms the implications of the fourth and asserts the efficacy of consciously controlled action in the world. When told that his regiment must charge the enemy, Henry "began to study the distance between him and the enemy. He made vague calculations. He saw that to be firm soldiers they must go forward." He leads the charge, urging his companions onward, unmindful of the danger around him. We should contrast the youth here to the youth whom we saw in the first three encounters. Here he is no longer simply an animal, reacting instinctively to a stimulus, but a man through whom Crane asserts the meaningfulness of human endeavor, by which he means conscious endeavor. As we might expect, throughout the course of Henry's development there are fewer and fewer comparisons of men with animals. During the fifth battle there are only two, neither of them degrading.

The fifth battle is Henry's only victorious encounter. Had he remained in the lines at the second battle, he would have participated in the victory accomplished by his regiment, but in terms of the over-all structure of the novel this would not have served Crane's ends. The victory achieved in the last battle becomes a kind of celebration of Henry's whole accomplishment, a culmination revealing that the direction of Henry's whole movement has some meaningful end. The resolution of his inward struggle has an effect on the outside world.

The other novel within *The Red Badge*, the one which

has as its theme that the nature of the universe is such that man can perform no meaningful action, is dependent upon the same external events as the one whose development we have been following, but its theme relies upon tone for its expression. The events of the novel, in other words, will not in themselves reveal the theme. Consequently that novel cannot be explored in the same way in which I have examined the novel having positive implications. Yet I believe that I have exhibited earlier ample evidence of its existence.

I believe that the problem of the ending of this novel came about essentially for two reasons. The first reason I admit to be speculative, not subject to "proof" in the same way that other opinions about literature can be "proved." It is my guess that Crane did not entirely approve of Henry's development into an individual capable of exercising the prerogatives, fulfilling the functions of an autonomous being. In *George's Mother* Crane reveals tremendous guilt feelings about his relationship with his own mother, and consequently George is the least sympathetic of the two characters. The death of Mrs. Kelcey at the end of the novel serves as a kind of *deus ex machina* allowing George to pursue his attempt to discover an identity unhampered by feelings of guilt toward a parent whom he must in a sense kill in the same way that the hero must kill the dragon which threatens at once to devour him and to put an end to his aspirations toward individual existence. The death of Mrs. Kelcey at the end of that novel is a means of circumventing the problem which Henry deals with in *The Red Badge* by simply leaving home. But Crane would not allow Henry's problem to be solved so easily. Crane was not at all sure that the development of the individual at the price of in some sense destroying the parent was worthwhile. Thus he was not at all sure that what Henry had to do to Mrs. Fleming was justified by the gain of being able to face the possibility of his own destruction. Since Crane had guilt feelings about his own movement toward autonomy, since he could not decide whether he himself was doing the best thing, he likewise could not decide whether Henry was. He admired Henry for responding to the call toward self-discovery, yet he hated him for overcoming his guilt feelings toward his mother.

The other reason for the problem of the novel, the one which I feel is more objectively demonstrable, amounts simply to considering the matter on a different level. There is a direct line of development in Crane's thought from *The Sullivan County Sketches*, through *Maggie*, to this novel. In the sketches we observed that Crane assumed man to be potentially free, though limited not by external forces, but by his own psychic being which until freed by conscious activity from the dominance of nature cannot exercise freedom of will. *Maggie*, on the other hand, is written from the premise that man is a determined creature having no control over what he is or what he does. The universe is such, Crane here assumes, that certain physical laws govern all phenomena; that essentially a decision made by a person is not different from the changing of the seasons. Crane was unable to relate these two ideas in such a way as to formulate them into a coherent view, a shortcoming resulting in tonal inconsistency so great as to prevent critics over the years from agreeing on what *The Red Badge* is about even in the most basic terms.

5

Some Other Tales of War: Heroism Re-examined

Although *The Red Badge* offers great difficulties of a certain kind to the interpreter who would ascertain its final meaning, many of Crane's other tales about war are not so perplexing. The works which I consider below are those which seem to me the best of their kind, and one of the primary reasons that they succeed as well as they do is that they indeed are not beset with problems of tone as is Crane's novel about a young man in war. These are all short works and consequently of lesser complexity. They all illustrate the distance Crane has come since *The Sullivan County Sketches*, and they suggest the potential which is realized in "The Open Boat."

It is difficult to withstand the temptation to use the short story "The Veteran" as evidence of Crane's intentions in *The Red Badge*, for this story shows us Henry Fleming, grown old, many years after the Civil War, a grandfather and a respected member of his community. We are led to infer from the story that Henry's war experiences were meaningful to him, that as a result of them he became better able to cope with life. But one should avoid this temptation, since "The Veteran" is another story, and Crane had no obligation in writing it to interpret the meaning of the earlier work. The tale is external evidence, and thus subject to the limitations of all other external evidence.

The story falls into two parts. The first section opens in a grocery store where a group of men have gathered who are currently questioning old Mr. Fleming about his war experiences. "You never was frightened much in them battles, was you?" [1] asks the grocer. Henry admits that he was indeed very much afraid, that he in fact ran away during the battle of Chancellorsville, but afterward "got kind of used to it." His little grandson is astonished that his magnificent grandfather would have been afraid, so astonished that he broods on the way home, obviously puzzled and disillusioned. This section, in that it tells us something of what Henry is like in later years as a result of his war experiences, prepares us for the section to follow where Henry unflinchingly demonstrates the courage he learned many years before.

The second section takes place on Henry's apparently large and prosperous farm. He has retired for the night, but is aroused by the noise of his farmhand, a Swede, who in his drunkenness has upset a kerosene lantern and started a fire in the barn. The old Henry dashes into the barn time after time and succeeds in rescuing the horses and cows, and eventually the Swede himself, who is disabled by a frightened cow. Henry accomplishes these things in spite of the fact that his whiskers and most of the hair on his head have been burned off, and his hip seems to have been injured by one of the horses. The Swede then reminds the group of fire fighters that two colts in the rear of the barn have been forgotten. Despite warnings that to return is sure death, Henry once again rushes into the barn only to be killed when the roof caves in.

> When the roof fell in, a great funnel of smoke swarmed toward the sky, as if the old man's mighty spirit, released from its body—a little bottle—had swelled like a genie of fable. The smoke was tinted rose-hue from the flames, and perhaps the unutterable midnights of the universe will have no power to daunt the color of this soul.

These lines, the concluding lines of the story, leave little doubt about whether in the perspective of the very nature of things courage is a desirable and worthwhile attribute. In *The Red Badge*, even after we have decided that Henry has committed heroic action, we are still faced with deciding whether courageous action is at all meaningful in a meaningless universe. "The Veteran" tells us that Henry's courageous response in the face of danger to himself is valuable and meaningful in itself although the answers to the ultimate questions about a man's relationship to the universe are shrouded in "unutterable midnights." But if "The Veteran" is an unambiguous statement about the meaning and value of courageous action, such is not the case with "A Mystery of Heroism," a fact which should deter any interpreter from reading the conclusions of "The Veteran" back into *The Red Badge*.

"A Mystery of Heroism" seems to suggest a conclusion opposite to that implied by the events of "The Veteran." Its ironic ending would apparently mean that courageous action is not meaningful in a universe whose nature is such that man's actions do not result in creating the world as he would have it. Is the exercise of courage worthwhile if the courageous actor is killed in the performance of his act or if his actions do not effect the particular end which he envisioned? My opinion is that the answer to that question is not different in "A Mystery of Heroism" from the opinion expressed in "The Veteran": the heroic act is meaningful whether or not it achieves its ends.

The title of the piece, "A Mystery of Heroism," is meant to imply that very question. Though Crane never answered the question, he never ceased asking it. In this particular case the object of Fred Collins' endeavor, a bucket of water, is in itself not very important in view of the fact that the men apparently could do without the water. But what is significant is that he accomplishes his task, which is to prove to himself and to his companions that he is capable of performing heroic action. The spilling of the water does not change the fact of the deed. Consequently, even in a world where nature herself does not recognize the meaning and value of heroism, it is a significant value if only because it fulfills some yearning in men. We should not read the concluding action of the story as indicating that Fred's accomplishment was a futile one since we know before he starts for the water that the water itself is not important. The "mystery of heroism" remains a mystery, yet the value of the heroic act remains undiminished. We see in "The Open Boat," where Crane deals at greater length with the same essential problem, that the strength and courage of the oiler are not any less to be valued because he of all the men on the dinghy drowns.

The two stories, "The Veteran" and "A Mystery of Heroism," are not as different as they might at first appear. The death of old Henry Fleming, in that he falls victim to circumstances over which he has no control, actually is structurally analogous to the dropping of the bucket at the end of the other story. But we are not inclined to give the same interpretation to that event because it does not seem so drastically ironic, and because the ending of that tale invites us to see Henry's exhibition of courage as being meaningful, even when seen against "the unutterable midnights of the universe."

Like "A Mystery of Heroism," "An Indiana Campaign" appears to be a story concerning much ado about nothing. Old Major Tom Boldin becomes the protector of his village when all the younger men march away to join the Union forces. One day when the Major sits sleeping on his bench beside the village tavern, a little boy frenziedly wakes him to report that a rebel, apparently a deserter, is in the area. The Major immediately gets his rifle and hurriedly sets out toward the wood where the rebel should be. The women, the children, and the old men of the village are frightened and excited because of the threat presented by the alleged intruder. The "rebel" turns out to be "ol' Milt' Jacoby," a village drunkard. "Well, yeh might have known," [2] say the women.

"An Indiana Campaign" is like "The Veteran" in that its central character is an old soldier who has solved the problems confronting Fred Collins in "A Mystery of Heroism." Neither of the old soldiers has the least hesitation about doing what he does. Neither has the same tenacious hold on life which the younger soldier has, though at the same time neither of the old men is simply foolhardy. All three of the stories assert that courageous action in the face of adversity is necessary and desirable despite the fact that it might or might not have some intimate relationship with the nature of things, that it might not accomplish what it was intended to accomplish.

"An Episode of War" describes the circumstances under which a man lost an arm. The lieutenant, as the central character is called, has nearly completed the job of painstakingly dividing into little squares the company's coffee ration when he is struck by a bullet which has emerged from a wood some distance away. He and his companions are shocked and surprised that the lieutenant should be wounded in this fashion. The situation seems odd to all involved because it is seldom that they have seen such a thing happen when they were not involved in battle, "when they had leisure to observe it." The lieutenant, thrust into a new role because he is wounded, proceeds unhurriedly toward the field hospital enabled by his wound to see with new eyes the fighting around him. Puzzled and bewildered, the lieutenant does not know how, as a wounded man, he should act when he meets others on the road. He eventually finds his way to a hospital where a seemingly contemptuous surgeon tells him to come along to have the arm taken care of. "I guess I won't have it amputated," says the lieutenant, losing his meekness, looking into the eyes of the doctor. "I won't amputate it." "Let go of me," cries the lieutenant, unwilling to enter the old schoolhouse which serves as a hospital. The lieutenant's arm is amputated. When he reaches home, he says to his sobbing relatives, "I don't suppose it matters so much as all that."

The theme of this story is that man is able to adjust with stoical resignation to the undeserved and uncontrollable adversity befalling him by seeing himself and his world in undistorted perspective. The lieutenant's task at the beginning of the story is a task involving the creation of order out of chaos. The division of the coffee into squares "astoundingly equal in size," the near "triumph in mathematics," stands in contrast to the random event

which stops the proceedings. Apparently the bullet was
not aimed at the lieutenant (since no more bullets come
and the men do not take cover), but merely happened to
hit him, an occurrence over which he hadn't the slightest
control. The swift alteration in the lieutenant's circumstances, the impingement of the chaotic upon the orderly,
is what shocks into silent amazement the group of men
waiting for their squads' supply of coffee.

After he is wounded, the lieutenant takes his sword in
his left hand, and holding it at the middle of its blade,
tries desperately to sheathe it. The instrument which only
moments before he had manipulated with such dexterity
in dividing the coffee has suddenly become unmanageable,
and he must depend upon another person to sheathe it for
him. An officer the lieutenant meets scolds him, saying
that he has not properly managed to care for his wound.
"The lieutenant hung his head, feeling, in this presence
[that of the other officer], that he did not know how to be
correctly wounded." He cannot understand how a man he
encounters near the hospital, much more seriously
wounded than he, can serenely smoke a pipe despite being
so close to dying. When he arrives at the hospital the
surgeon, whom he sees as a figure of authority, takes
charge of him, saying, at one point, "Come along. Don't
be a baby." The lieutenant has the problem of recognizing
that though his wound has transformed his role, his new
role should not be that one stemming from the fact of his
dependence on those around him, but a role resulting
from his own individual awareness of the requirements
necessary for dealing with his life.

There are two views of the wounded man presented in
the tale, one that of soldiers, and the other the view of the
surgeon. Of the soldiers' view Crane says,

> A wound gives strange dignity to him who bears it. Well
> men shy from this new and terrible majesty. It is as if the
> wounded man's hand is upon the curtain which hangs
> before the revelations of all existence—the meaning of ants,
> potentates, wars, cities, sunshine, snow, a feather dropped
> from a bird's wing; and the power of it sheds radiance upon

a bloody form, and makes the other men understand sometimes that they are little.

This way of regarding the lieutenant causes him to see
himself as those others see him. Their projection of what
he is defines for him how to act. He feels that he doesn't
know how to act, yet the deference with which he is
treated by soldiers causes him to be dependent, to feel
that his wound does indeed separate him from other men.
But in contrast to the way soldiers view the wounded
officer, the surgeon looks impersonally upon him. When
the surgeon responds in a manner contrary to the sympathetic response of others, the lieutenant sees his attitude
as being contemptuous whereas it is actually only impersonal. The man who sits outside the hospital seriously
wounded and dying, yet serenely smoking a pipe, has the
same attitude as the doctor and the same attitude the
lieutenant learns between the time of the amputation and
the conclusion of the story, for the final lines echo not the
attitude expressed by the sympathetic gestures of other
soldiers, but the attitude of the dying man and the surgeon, "I don't suppose it matters so much as all that."
The stoical indifference manifest in the last line of the
story stems from the lieutenant's undistorted view of himself in relation to the world, and stands in sharp contrast
to the view he has when he is first wounded, when the
wound matters a great deal. The lieutenant knows at the
end of the story that in a world where such a thing
happens nothing "matters so much as all that."

Crane wrote other tales of the Civil War, but none are
so successful as these. Those tales which succeed best seem
to be those which end on an ironic note. Those least
successful are those lacking consistent focus, and which, at
the same time, do not end ironically. This should suggest
a relationship between Crane's use of the ironic ending
and the problem of focus. And so there is. Crane's ironic
endings work well because they provide an organizational
center giving meaning to the events preceding them. The
ironic ending, when it works well, points out and defines

the specific concern of the tale, indicating at the same time the author's attitude toward that matter.

One of the central difficulties of "The Little Regiment" is its improper focus. The title of the story itself hints at the problem, for the story is not concerned with the regiment, but with two men who could be in any regiment at all. Nothing about this particular group makes it important to this story about two brothers, Dan and Billie, who though constantly aggressive and hostile toward each other, hold deep mutual affection. The problem of focus arises when Crane describes in great detail the movements and the surroundings of the whole regiment without relating these things to a central theme.

"The Little Regiment" is a sentimental tale during the course of which little attention is given to plot or character. It intends to engender a stock response from its readers in the same way that "A Grey Sleeve" and "Three Miraculous Soldiers," two other tales about the Civil War, intend to do. "A Grey Sleeve" is about a Northern officer who is deeply attracted to a Southern girl after his patrol enters her house to search for the wearer of the grey sleeve one of the soldiers saw in the window. The other story is about a Southern girl who is able to feel great sympathy toward a Northern soldier despite the fact that she helps four Southerners to escape from Northern forces. Each story means to suggest that the affections of the heart are superior to political loyalty, a proposition, which though ultimately true and desirable, is likely to be merely sentimental, given the context of our world.

Although Crane's concern with the Civil War yielded some excellent tales, his direct involvement with the Spanish American War yielded not one tale of outstanding merit,[3] an ironical circumstance if we consider the value which he placed on experience. Yet some of these tales are interesting for various reasons, though they are for the most part only surface accounts of human experience, some being merely reportorial accounts of Crane's impressions during his Cuban adventure.

"Marines Signalling Under Fire," for example, is not

actually a tale at all, but a piece attempting to describe the danger which signal corpsmen faced during the fighting in Cuba. At night they signaled by means of lanterns, during the day with flags. In order to be seen by the persons to whom they were signaling they often exposed themselves to the enemy who blasted away at them. Crane would of course be impressed by the great courage these men exhibited. He reveals great admiration for an officer who insisted on standing up with a corpsman behind the lanterns, thus participating in the danger.

Humorous and well-written among these tales is one called "The Sergeant's Private Madhouse." Forty men are occupying an isolated outpost surrounded by hostile Cubans loyal to Spain. Attacked, the forty marines fight furiously, but they discover that their ammunition is running low. At the point at which a charge by the enemy would mean certain defeat and even death at the hands of an enemy who takes no prisoners, Dryden, a battle-fatigued soldier, sings out in a loud voice, "While shepherds watched their flocks by night . . ." Both sides stop firing, amazed that such a thing should occur. The Cubans do not attack again, and Dryden has saved his group.

"The Sergeant's Private Madhouse" is about a situation rather than a character. Having no central character, it shows what happens to be a group of men after the occurrence of a fortuitous event responsible for their being saved. Every character is at the end just as we found him at the beginning. Though the tale has no great significance beyond suggesting the irony often occurring in human existence, it is a well-contrived piece. Dryden's stopping the attack is no *deus ex machina*, but an event made quite probable by what has proceeded. Slight though the ideational content may be, Crane here has his materials well in hand, seeming aware at each moment of what he intends to do.

"The Clan of No-Name" is structurally more complex than most of Crane's short fiction usually is. It is a framed story, the first and last sections dealing with Margharita, a girl who at the beginning loves Manolo, the focal charac-

ter, but at the end, after his death, marries Mr. Smith, a
weak and fearful admirer over whose emotions she exercises firm control. The main action of the story, which
takes place in Cuba, centers around the attempt of an
expedition to transport supplies through the Spanish lines.
To achieve this it is necessary that a group of men engage
the enemy, stalling them until the expeditionary force is
well on its way. A part of the insurgent group engages the
blockhouse; the others engage the much larger Spanish
force on the road. The two insurgent groups eventually
join and fight a rearguard action to allow the larger expeditionary force time to escape. The expedition succeeds, but
most if not all of the protectors are killed.

Manolo has been sent to aid the right side of the
retreating insurgent line. He knows that if he holds his
position, he will be killed, yet he does hold it because he
feels that he must.

> He knew that he was trusting himself into a trap whose
> door, once closed, opened only when the black hand
> knocked; and every part of him seemed to be in panic-
> stricken revolt. But something controlled him; something
> moved him inexorably in one direction; he perfectly under-
> stood, but he was only sad, sad with a serene dignity, with
> the countenance of a mournful young prince. He was of a
> kind—that seemed to be it; and the men of his kind, on
> peak or plain, from the dark northern ice-fields to the hot
> wet jungles, through all wine and want, through all lies and
> unfamiliar truth, dark or light—the men of his kind were
> governed by their gods, and each man knew the law and yet
> could not give tongue to it, but it was the law; and if the
> spirits of the men of his kind were all sitting in critical
> judgment upon him even then in the sky, he could not
> have bettered his conduct; he needs must obey the law, and
> always with the law there is only one way. But from peak to
> plain, from dark northern ice-fields and hot wet jungles,
> through wine and want, through all lies and unfamiliar
> truth, dark or light, he heard breathed to him the approval
> and benediction of his brethren.

This eloquent statement makes clear a matter which
Crane seems to have implied in many places before, that

courage is its own justification for being. Just as here it really makes no difference that Margharita is so quickly able to forget her attachment to Manolo, to burn his picture and to accept the proposal of Mr. Smith, so in other tales, "A Mystery of Heroism," "The Veteran," "An Indiana Campaign," it makes no difference in the final analysis that the act of courage may fail in preserving one or in achieving his intentions. One does what he must do despite the vicissitudes of human existence. This is the answer to the riddle which appears as the epigraph to "The Clan of No-Name."

> Unwind my riddle.
> Cruel as hawks the hours fly;
> Wounded men seldom come home to die;
> The hard waves see an arm flung high;
> Scorn hits strong because of a lie;
> Yet there exists a mystic tie.
> Unwind my riddle.

In form and style "The Clan of No-Name" is different from any story that Crane ever wrote. The complexity of its structure, its rearrangement of chronology, its broad spatial sweep allowing us to see the action from the points of view of all the groups involved and finally from the point of view of one character, are, taken together, quite atypical of Crane's work. Also atypical is the involuted and rehetorical style of the prose passage quoted above, a style interwined throughout the story with the style more typically Crane's.

Other pieces about war are "Death and the Child," which takes place during the Greco-Turkish War, "Ol' Bennet and the Indians," a Revolutionary episode, and "The Upturned Face," the last of four stories about an imaginary regiment, The Kicking Twelfth, in an imaginary place fighting an imaginary battle.

"Death and the Child" is a good story, but not among the best of the tales Crane wrote about war. It is the story of a Greek reporter, Peza, come from Italy, whose patriotic fervor is aroused when he nears battle. He decides he wants to fight. After finding his way to the front lines, he finds that he cannot face death. Peza, until the time that he discovers this has felt that he knew all about war. He is an educated man, who writes sonnets, but has apparently had most of his experience of life in his head rather than in actuality. In the story he is the negative force in the sense that his particular way of acting is felt by the author to be undesirable when it is contrasted with the positive forces in the short story, those centers of value which suggest a better way of acting than his. These two centers of value are the experienced soldiers whom Peza encounters at the front, and the child who overlooks the battle from a high hill. Now if the story is to be consistent, there should be some relationship between these two centers. That is, through imitation or adoption of the values of either he should be able to be courageous in the face of death. From the soldiers he might learn to control his conduct by strict observance of decorum as he observes the officers control themselves, or he might learn simply to face up to what is required of him as the enlisted peasants do. But what could he learn from the child?

Supposedly he could learn the child's "primitive courage." But I find it doubtful that a child is courageous in the way that an adult is. If we wish to define courage as unknowingness, then we can say that the child is courageous as "the mountains, the sky, and the sea" are courageous. Then courage becomes unconsciousness. Surely the men involved in the battle in this story are not unconscious. Though there are undoubtedly worthwhile values to be found in childhood, one of those values is not courage. In fact the man who would be courageous must forsake the values of childhood in order to discover values more compatible with his ends. To call the child "sovereign" where courage is required, as Crane does, is merely to be sentimental.

Just as it seems odd and unusual to see Crane adopt the primitivistic stance of "Death and the Child," so likewise it is peculiar to see him tell a story from the point of view of the first person as "Ol' Bennet and the Indians" is told.

This tale falls into two main parts. The first involves the narrator himself, Ol' Bennet's sixteen-year-old son, who, one morning during a time when their Wyoming Valley is threatened by Indians and British troops, is told by his father, "Son, go and fight."

Ol' Bennet is feared by the Indians in the territory because of his firmness toward them. Like an Old Testament prophet, he stands firm and sure against the world, never doubting his decisions, never changing his mind, ruling his family with an iron hand. Quite reasonably, the son at sixteen is not able to cope with the world in the same fashion. He is not yet sufficiently strong to sustain himself. Consequently, after fleeing during his first battle with the Indians he says, "I set out for home. I set out for home in that perfect spirit of dependence which I had always felt toward my father and mother. . . . The whole shame of the business came upon me suddenly. 'Father,' I choked out, 'we have been beaten.' 'Ay,' said he, 'I expected it.' " The fact that the son does not at all question the ways of the father causes him to be treated with some irony, but the gentlest irony. Though Crane contrasts the effectiveness with which the two are able to deal with the world, he does not hold the boy accountable for his lesser ability, as when the boy naïvely observes of the father, "If people had thoroughly known my father, he would have had no enemies. . . . If people wished his good opinion they only had to do exactly as he did, and to have his views."

The point of view with which this story is told avoids many of the difficulties of style which are likely to be present even when Crane is at his best. But this is a mixed blessing since many of his best effects have come about when he attempts to reach beyond the usual, the traditional ways of expression. The point of view limits the range of metaphor and diction to the expression possible to a sixteen-year-old country lad, and the whole story succeeds as well as it does largely because Crane's feelings toward the boy and toward his father are clear to him. It is interesting to note that Crane was able to treat this boy, whose role is clearly defined for him by his father, with great clarity of feeling, while his attitude toward such characters as George Kelcey and Henry Fleming, those fatherless boys, was ambivalent. This character, who doesn't strive against authority, seems clearly favored of the three, largely because Crane achieves a degree of aesthetic distance much greater than in the works involving the other two characters, thus allowing him more objectivity.

Death is the subject of one of Crane's shortest and most successful war stories, "The Upturned Face," the last of four stories about a regiment, The Kicking Twelfth, a part of the imaginary Spitzbergen army. The "plot" of the story is this: two officers, with the help of two privates, bury a fellow officer. But the concern of the story is not so much with the action itself as with the reactions of the two officers to the situation. Timothy Lean wants to bury the body of their comrade, while the adjutant, his superior, suggests that the body be left despite the fact that they are about to retreat. Timothy is directed by a sense of duty, not to the dead as such, but to a dear friend, the dead man apparently having been a friend of both men.

Like Henry Fleming in the scene in *The Red Badge* depicting the death of Jim Conklin, these two men identify closely with the victim. But unlike Henry, they seem awed not by the possibility of their own death so much as by the acutely impinging awareness of the finality of death. Though bullets are flying close to them, the enemy having found the range of the company, and one of the privates is wounded while filling in the grave, neither Timothy nor the adjutant shrinks from the task out of fear of bodily harm. What they cannot accept at the moment is the clear and present existential necessity of realizing the finality of death, a problem to these men, who have seen many dead bodies, because the corpse is of an intimate friend whom they must bury with their own hands.

Both men respond similarly in that they identify with the dead man, yet they differ in their desire and ability to recognize the finality of death. The adjutant from the beginning wants nothing to do with the matter, or at least as little as possible. He makes Timothy search the body for belongings although Timothy is less than anxious to do so. When the grave is finished, the adjutant, purely out of nervous anxiety, laughs weirdly, saying humorously, "I suppose we had best tumble him in." The body is tumbled into the grave, both men being careful to handle the clothing and not touch the corpse itself. They are relieved once they have got that far. The adjutant suggests that some words be said over the corpse "while he can hear us," suggesting he is not yet thoroughly convinced that the man is dead. Nor is Timothy, who feels immense relief when the soldier, after holding the soil in his shovel, poised above the corpse, empties it on the feet of the dead man rather than on the face which "looked keenly out from the grave." When the man with the shovel is wounded, Timothy undertakes the task of filling the grave. The adjutant yet feels that it would have been better to leave the body. "Perhaps we have been wrong," he says. "It might have been better if we hadn't buried him just at this time. Of course, if we advance tomorrow the body would have been . . ." "Damn you," Lean says, "shut your mouth." It is not fear that prompts this exchange, but the inability of the adjutant to accept as fact that the man is dead in opposition to Lean's sense of duty to their mutual friend, a sense of duty so strong as to force him to face the finality of death. Soon the grave is filled in except for the area surrounding the face. So closely have these two identified with the dead man that they feel that they are themselves having their faces covered with that last shovelful of earth. When his face is finally covered, the dead man will have ceased to exist for the two officers with a finality greater than that brought about by the bullet which killed him. Had it not been for the sense of duty which Timothy felt, the man would not have been buried, for neither Lean nor the adjutant can face easily the fact of the actual end of this man.

"The Upturned Face" differs from most of Crane's pieces about death in that it goes beyond the simple animal aversion to physical destruction, to deal with a more subtle problem. These men apparently do not have the fear of being killed or wounded which many in Crane's fiction have. Even when the soldier filling in the grave is wounded, the two officers exhibit no fear for their personal safety. Also there is no reliance in this story on the stock response toward death elicited by horrifying descriptions of a bloody and torn body or the grotesque attitudes which the dead sometimes assume.

The commonplace of Crane criticism, that he is better able to handle shorter than longer forms of fiction, is borne out by the tales about war, the best of which I have dealt with here. The others, those I consider less successful, fail primarily for two reasons: they are not purely fiction, being transcripts of Crane's actual experience, unshaped by the creative imagination; or they are works which are sentimental, following popular formulas of fiction in plot and character. Seldom, however, do these pieces fail primarily because of their point of view or because of their tone. Since these pieces were written after *The Red Badge*, we may infer that Crane learned to control to some degree his point of view and tone, but we will see that this is not consistently so, that from time to time, especially in the longer stories, he fell back into the same difficulty.

6

"The Blue Hotel"
and Other Tales of the Woolly West [1]

Though "The Blue Hotel" has been accounted one of the best things that Crane did, the meaning of that perform- ance has been as variously interpreted as the meaning of *The Red Badge*. A number of critics have seen the tale as having as its central theme the brotherhood of man: against a universe which in its indifference seems hostile and malevolent, man can only maintain order and mean- ing in his life if he recognizes and fulfills his responsibility as a link in "the magnetic chain of humanity." Some have seen the tale as meaning we are determined creatures, that the complexity of human behavior is so great and our knowledge of what goes on around us so imperfect that we have no control over our destinies when we are involved with other human beings. If the former statement is the theme, then we are all responsible to and for each other. If the latter, then no one is responsible. Needless to say, these two possibilities are antithetical. Yet there seems to be in the story evidence sufficiently strong to have demon- strated to nearly all critics the truth of one of these propositions. The best support of either position is to be found in the conclusion.

Let us assume for the time being that the story intends to point out that we are determined creatures, victims of an inexorable necessity, exercising no control over our fate. What happens when we examine the famous speech of the Easterner near the end of the story?

> We are all in it! This poor gambler isn't even a noun. He is a kind of adverb. Every sin is the result of a collaboration.

We, five of us, have collaborated in the murder of this Swede. Usually there are from a dozen to forty women really involved in every murder, but in this case it seems to be only five men—you, I, Johnnie, old Scully; and that fool of an unfortunate gambler came merely as a culmination, the apex of a human movement and gets all the punishment.[2]

The analogy likening the gambler to a part of a syntactical structure, and to a modifying word rather than to a word determining basic meaning, like a noun or verb, suggests that the gambler had little control over his fate and the Swede even less. As an adverb he is meaningless until he becomes attached to some verb, adjective, or other adverb which will allow him a function. It is quite clear in retrospect that had the events occurring at the hotel happened differently, then the gambler most likely would not have been intimidated by the Swede and would not have killed him. The gambler had absolutely no control over what happened at the hotel and in this sense came "merely as a culmination, the apex of a human movement and got all the punishment." The Swede dies because of his limited and imperfect knowledge. Had he chosen to grab any man at the table but the gambler, he probably would not have been murdered. It would seem, as one critic has so ably put it, that Crane "has absolutely shown that men's wills do not control their destinies."[3]

But what happens if we look at that last section from the point of view of one who would see the meaning of the tale as primarily involving the brotherhood of man theme? First of all it is quite obvious that regardless of Crane's intentions the Easterner intends to say that all men share the burden of responsibility for evil, that faced by a universe which has no regard for him, man must recognize the necessity of his involvement with other men. Seen from this vantage point, the Easterner's statement, "The Swede might not have been killed if everything had been square," implies the possibility of the action turning out differently from the way it did. When the Easterner further says, "Johnnie was cheating. I saw him . . . . And

I refused to stand up and be a man. I let the Swede fight it out alone. And you—you were simply puffing around the place and wanting to fight. And then old Scully himself! We are all in it," he means to indicate responsibility, to point out the guilty. It is also quite clear here that the cowboy, whose experience and sensibilities are quite limited, is intended to present the less satisfactory point of view toward the events preceding the last scene. He fails completely to comprehend the meaning of the Easterner's statement about the complicity of the five men in the murder of the Swede. "Well, I didn't do anythin', did I?" he asks naïvely. It seems clear enough that the answer to the cowboy's question would be a restatement of what the Easterner has said already, that men have responsibility toward each other; hence the theme of the brotherhood of man.

Now if the Easterner's statements interpret truly the preceding action as indicating the necessity of human beings acting responsibly toward each other, and if one feels that the story shows "that men's wills do not control their destinies," then some kind of adjustment must be made between the two alternatives since they are mutually exclusive. One way of dealing with the problem is by discounting the Easterner's comments at the end of the story. This to me seems impossible because I detect nothing there which would indicate a disparity between the attitudes expressed by the Easterner and Crane's attitudes. One anxious critic goes so far as to say that "the Easterner's speech is swelling with self-importance and half-truth." [4] This seems to me a terribly erroneous reading of the last section, a reading creating far more problems than it solves because we have then to deal with the cowboy's reaction to the Easterner's speech and certainly Crane's attitude is not the same as the cowboy's. There is no reason to suspect that the Easterner interprets the preceding events wrongly.

Another way of "proving" that the theme of the story is not the brotherhood theme is by dismissing the final section as being "tacked on." The inadequacy of the theory that the conclusion is "tacked on" becomes immediately apparent when we consider the extent to which it has been prepared for by the preceding action. Certainly it was necessary, if Crane's intention—whatever that was—were to be fulfilled, that the reader know that Johnnie had in fact cheated in the card game. Though we are surprised to learn this, it is not a shock if we remember that at the beginning of the story, when Scully returns to the hotel with the new guests, Johnnie is playing cards with a farmer. The two are arguing. Shortly afterwards when they are playing High-Five, the game being played later when Johnnie is accused of cheating, the play is again stopped by an argument. We do not *know* what the two are arguing about, but it is not difficult to imagine that the farmer had seen Johnnie cheat, but, knowing the code of the West, did not dare accuse him directly.

It ought also be considered that the character of the Easterner is such that he might very well keep silent about seeing Johnnie cheat. He is a meek man. It is he who is most affected by the cold, and it is he who attempts to prevent the fight between Johnnie and the Swede. He is the least outspoken among the men in the story, and he is the least strongly moved by the curious responses of the Swede. His primary intention seems to be to avoid conflict of any kind. Too, he is shown to be a sensitive enough individual that it might indeed occur to him that he and the others are to some degree responsible for the outcome of the central action of the tale.

Those who dismiss the conclusion are having their cake and eating it too, because prior to the last section there is little to suggest determinism, or that "men's wills do not control their destinies." These critics have taken one of the possible interpretations of the last section, applied it to the tale, then dismissed the last section. The error comes about as a result of our too great willingness to see a kind of consistency in Crane's work which really isn't there. His work is as varied as it could possibly be. Because we see determinism in some of his earlier work, we should not expect to find it in everything he did. He worked this problem out in *Maggie* and *The Red Badge* and never returned to it again. Those critics who have seen fit to give support to the assumption that "The Blue Hotel" shows that men do not control their destinies have little more than the weather to point to as proof of their claim. They feel apparently that since the weather serves as such a constricting force on the activities of men it determines men's actions rather than limits them. The only other support for this position prior to the concluding section is the fact that there exists a causal relation between what happened at the hotel and the Swede's death. It would seem that the murder was an act of necessity, inevitable. But is this really saying any more than that in fiction plot usually proceeds from character? Is it not true that in every worthwhile piece of fiction ever written there is a causal relation between character and event? In the same manner that we can show that the Swede's death occurs out of necessity we can show that most fiction is deterministic. But this is no more satisfactory than are those arguments which intend to prove that we in life are determined creatures.

On the other hand the brotherhood theme is developed during the course of the narrative, but in a way different from the Easterner's interpretation of the meaning of what has occurred. The Easterner suggests that each of us should be his brother's keeper, yet the story implies that the view is not in itself an adequate solution if we mean by "adequate solution" whatever would have prevented the Swede's death. Scully does all within the range of his possibilities to protect the Swede, to alleviate his fears, to prevent conflict between him and the other men. Yet the conflict occurs and the Swede is eventually murdered. Even after the Swede has had a drink and has become most obnoxious Scully admits by his manner "his responsibility for the Swede's new view point." It is only when Scully is exasperated beyond his endurance that he turns against the Swede. Before that point his intentions have been the very best, and he acts as well as one whose intentions are good can act, given the limitations of his knowledge.

Up to the point of the concluding section the brotherhood theme is developed in a kind of obverse manner.

Though a reader might conclude prior to that section that men should recognize the necessity of mutual involvement, he is not likely to see, as the Easterner sees, that "we are all in it," that the responsibility for the Swede's death is a social responsibility extending even beyond the group immediately involved in the circumstances leading up to the event. Up to the final section Crane's attitude toward him leads us to believe that the responsibility for his death rests with the Swede alone; we are then shown the other side of the coin when the complicity of the others is revealed, especially that of Johnnie and the Easterner.

The tone of the first eight sections indicates that Crane has very little sympathy for the Swede. Whereas his attitude toward Henry Fleming is consistently ambivalent, his attitude toward the Swede is untempered by any charitable feeling. As readers our attitude toward the Swede is likely to be the same as Crane's. We are led by Crane to judge the Swede negatively because he exhibits no redeeming qualities. His view of his situation and of other people is completely distorted, his reactions odd and perverse. Until he takes the first drink of whiskey, he, like so many of Crane's other characters, is entirely at the mercy of his own distorted view of himself and his surroundings. Such a fearful person as he cannot function in the world even moderately well. After the drink of whiskey in Scully's upstairs room, his bravado is proportionately as great as his fear had been before. And like that fear, it too is founded on a distortion of reality. Not only is his courage false courage, a temporary courage which will last only as long as his inebriation, but it also is dependent upon his erroneous notion that he has risen superior to the situation he saw in the beginning, that he has come to manipulate those who only moments before intended to murder him. Distortion becomes compounded upon distortion. In his cups he becomes totally obnoxious, intimidating everyone, and revealing rudeness, crudity, vulgarity, and cruelty so great as to render sympathetic judgment of him extremely difficult if not impossible.

In order to arrive at a statement of the theme of "The

Blue Hotel" it is necessary to determine whether the Swede is representative of mankind, for if he is, this story is a more bitterly satirical indictment of man than has heretofore been recognized. There are two places in the text implying that he is. One is the famous passage in the eighth section of the story.

> He might have been in a deserted village. We picture the world as thick with conquering and elate humanity, but here, with the bugles of the tempest pealing, it was hard to imagine a peopled earth. One viewed the existence of man then as a marvel, and conceded a glamor of wonder to these lice which were caused to cling to a whirling, fire-smitten, ice-locked, disease-stricken, space-lost bulb. The conceit of man was explained by this storm to be the very engine of life. One was a coxcomb not to die in it. However, the Swede found a saloon.

The whole passage is a comment on the Swede and a further manifestation of the author's negative attitude toward him. The irony is intended to display the degree to which the Swede's image of himself is out of touch with things as they are. But the feeling directed toward the Swede spills over onto mankind as a whole, endowing him with a conceit and a blindness equal to those of the Swede. The two levels of meaning in this passage are at odds. When Crane says, "One was a coxcomb not to die in it," he means both that one who has separated himself from mankind and attempts to face alone the universe such as it is has little chance of survival (compare Harry Morgan's statement in *To Have and to Have Not*, a man alone has little chance), and that men are fools to attempt to survive in an indifferent universe. The former statement is supported by what has gone before, the latter isn't. What has gone before suggests that man's survival depends not on conceit, but on his involvement in the human community. The passage is an outstanding bit of nihilistic rhetoric which unfortunately interferes with the focus of the story.

The other passage, implying that the Swede is representative of mankind and that his problems should be seen as the problems of mankind, describes the stabbing of the Swede by the gambler.

> There was a great tumult, and then was seen a long blade in the hand of the gambler. It shot forward, and a human body, this citadel of virtue, wisdom, power, was pierced as easily as if it had been a melon.

It is not only the Swede's body which is seen ironically as a "citadel of virtue, wisdom, power," but any human body is subject to the irony of the passage. Again the generalization is not supported by what has heretofore occurred. The statement would be justified were it applicable to the Swede alone, whose false and distorted image of himself has caused him to feel as though he were a superior person. But as it is, the central events of the tale have not indicated that men in general have a similarly distorted image of self. The last line of the section, "This registers the amount of your purchase," must certainly refer only to the Swede, for his demise has occurred largely because of his character. In this story Crane desires to express negative, hostile feelings toward mankind, but these emerge only at specific points in the tale and are not integrated within the plot. He associates these venomous feelings with the Swede because he is the person Crane dislikes most in the story, but since the Swede has problems peculiar to himself, different from the problems of anyone else in the story, since he stands so much apart in his individuality, we have no reason, so far as achieved content is concerned, to consider him representative of mankind.

The central movement of "The Blue Hotel" traces the development and eventual outcome of the Swede's isolation from other men, his retreat away from the world into a world of his own making, a world in which he feels himself to be one who manipulates his environment rather than being manipulated by it. From the very beginning the rather bizarre reactions of the Swede to his situation set him apart from the other men in the hotel. His shrill, nearly hysterical laughter begins to unite the others with the bond of normalcy in the face of the aberrant behavior of the Swede. He evokes an increasingly hostile response from Johnnie and the cowboy, who find themselves unable to cope with the situation.

At every turn the Swede interprets external events in the light of his preconceived notion of what the West and Westerners are like. The hostility engendered in Johnnie and the cowboy can only be a sign that they intend to kill him. The Easterner's refusal to see the situation as he sees it can only mean that the Easterner is part of the conspiracy against him. When Scully follows him upstairs to his room, appearing at the door with his face lightened and enshadowed by the lamp he carries, he appears to the Swede like a murderer. Mistakenly considering himself alone and an outcast from the society of men, he indeed becomes just that, creating a world in which he is powerless and a victim of the machinations of others. Nothing the good-intentioned Scully can do or say can shake the Swede's fixed idea.

After the Swede has taken the first drink from Scully, he becomes intoxicated with drink and with power, feeling that he is at last in control of the threatening situation. It is not that he sees the others truly, that he sees that they do not intend to murder him; rather he feels in control of these potential murderers. But by his overbearingness and aggressiveness he manages further to isolate himself from the others in whom he has already aroused suspicion and antagonism by the strangeness of his responses. When finally he accuses Johnnie of cheating, he severs himself entirely from the group. He welcomes the chance to avenge himself on these enemies by thrashing one of their number. After the fight is over and the Swede has vanquished his opponent, he feels that his overweening confidence has been vindicated: "There was a splendor of isolation in his situation at this time which the Easterner felt once when, lifting his eyes from the man on the ground, he beheld that mysterious and lonely figure, waiting." Later, having left the hotel, the Swede finds pleasure in the wind and driving snow, feeling that his new-found strength is so great that he can survive in isolation. He feels invincible against the powers of both man and nature. "Yes, I like this weather. I like it. It suits me," he says in contrast to the reaction of the Easterner after the fight, who rushes in to the stove, nearly daring "to embrace the glowing iron."

From the heights of his towering pride the Swede looks down upon men, and being unable to distinguish his similarity to them, feels free of the limitations imposed on men by the nature of things. Like Icarus, who, intoxicated with the dizzying wine of seemingly unconstrained flight, flew too near to the sun and, his wings destroyed, tumbled to his death in the sea, the Swede falls, stabbed by the gambler, and supremely "astonished" that such a thing could happen to him.

Far from being "tacked on" or a distorted interpretation of the preceding action, the final section of "The Blue Hotel" complements what has gone before. We learn in the first eight sections that the Swede is primarily responsible for his own death, that it occurs as a result of his character. The last section rounds out the tale by revealing the complicity of others in the event. The view of the Easterner is limited (but not distorted) because in his analysis he fails to include the Swede himself as one of those responsible. But we are misreading the tale if we take the Easterner's interpretation of the action to mean that the Swede is absolved from responsibility, that he had no other choices to make. That is, unless one wishes to engage in the arguments about determinism in life, for there is no more in the tale to suggest that the Swede is determined than there is to suggest that life is determined.

We can account for the negative attitude of the author toward the Swede by reference to the theme of the story: against a universe which in its indifference seems hostile and malevolent, man can only maintain order and meaning in this life if he recognizes and fulfills his responsibility as a link in "the magnetic chain of humanity." The point is that no matter how reprehensible the Swede was, there are others, who, though not equally as guilty as the gambler, are nonetheless stained. The tale could easily have been about the Easterner, about a sensitive and well-meaning man, whose inability to be brave at a critical moment causes him to be involved in an act which he himself would never commit, he having failed to fulfill a responsibility not always easily fulfilled. Like the author, he too sided against the Swede, yet he does not attempt to deny his involvement in the murder.

Still the problem of tone which we have seen in others of Crane's works occurs in regard to his attitude toward the Swede. The problem is somewhat different here, but is nonetheless the cause of a great defect in the story. Crane's attitude toward the Swede is too harsh. One does not regret that the Swede cannot be a tragic figure since he is among the worst of mankind as Crane has created him. One might feel, however, that a reader would be more in sympathy with the Easterner's interpretation of the affair if he were not asked to forget so quickly the great degree to which the Swede is responsible for his own death. When we are told that his death "registers the amount of his purchase," we are likely to agree that such an unworthy person did indeed get what was coming to him. It is difficult to conceive of what the Easterner calls a "sin" in the story as being less than the fulfillment of poetic justice. Because Crane has been so harsh in his judgment of the Swede, we are likely to feel as the cowboy feels, "He the gambler don't deserve none of it for killin' who he did." It is an error in execution that our sympathies should be with the Easterner and not at all with the Swede, who, after all, is dead. We should be sorry that he is dead, but who is?

Seen in the perspective of the rest of Crane's work, "The Blue Hotel" is not so far removed from those stories we have examined as might be supposed. At the beginning of the story the Swede's problems are not entirely different from the problems faced by the little man of *The Sullivan County Sketches*, by George Kelcey of *George's Mother*, nor by Henry Fleming. Each of these characters has the problem of discovering an identity, of freeing himself from constricting influences (fear, parental authority, certain natural forces requiring will to overcome) and thus arriving at a position allowing him to find out his own strengths and limitations, to find his own place in the world and his own relation to the cosmos. The Swede, as we first see him, is so out of control of himself that he is nearly hysterical. As the victim of his fear, he is incapable of acting freely; he is manipulated by his fear of death. In this sense the Swede is every character in Crane's fiction whom we have seen so far who has been afraid of dying, every character who, because he is psychically encumbered in one way or another, is ineffectual in the world, and thereby unable to deal with that world.

But "The Blue Hotel" differs in its treatment of this character in some very important respects. With other characters like the Swede, notably Henry Fleming and George Kelcey, Crane has shown an essential concern with their development from that state in which the individual has only the most limited control over what he is and does, to a more desired state where the individual can function as freely as human beings can function through the exercise of conscious will. From nonconsciousness (will-lessness) to consciousness (wilfulness). But here, Crane is not concerned with the matter of development. In fact he short-circuits the movement from one state to the other by simply having the Swede take a drink. After taking a drink the Swede loses all fear.

Now we saw in another story which Crane wrote, "The Duel That Was Not Fought," an examination of the question, is courage untempered by discretion meaningful? His concentration on this question precluded the necessity of concern for the development of his character to a state of fearlessness. If we look at "The Blue Hotel" from this point of view, another level of meaning emerges: courage untempered by discretion is not valuable, nor is discretion (the Easterner is discreet in not backing up the Swede's charge against Johnnie) worthwhile if it replaces courage. If these two alternatives are viewed in relation to the ideal of mutual responsibility among men, we see that neither is a responsible attitude, and we find ourselves not very far distant from the level of meaning discussed in the preceding section. All in all "The Blue Hotel" parallels most of the work discussed up to this point having to do with the multifarious ramifications of the ideal of courage as it relates to the problems of living in this world.

It is a good rule of thumb to doubt an author's judgment of the quality of his own work. Crane felt "A Man and Some Others" to be one of the best things he had done, and Joseph Conrad agreed, placing the story above even "The Open Boat." " 'A Man and Some Others' is the best of the two," Conrad commented, "but the boat thing interested me more." [5] Though I would not agree that this story is better than "The Open Boat," I would class it among Crane's best work, agreeing in part with the author's judgment. This tale of the Mexican mesa is not one which is anthologized, an odd phenomenon, if my judgment of its value is sound, since it is so typical of Crane.

The plot itself reveals how typical of Crane's work this story is. The young stranger is like the little man, like Henry Fleming, and like George Kelcey in that he is an innocent, who has yet to be tempered in the fire of experience. Like those earlier characters, he has yet to gain the psychic freedom necessary to establish his identity. In one sense "A Man and Some Others" is *The Red Badge of Courage* in miniature, but unlike the novel, it is not beset with the same problems of ambivalence of feeling. The similarity is apparent if one is aware that the focus in the story is on the young stranger rather than on Bill, the sheepherder, who during the course of his life has been involved in many conflicts where life or death was at stake. The action shows that the young stranger is the one who is changed by the events that occur. Bill's character is fixed. Had the stranger not been in the story, it would have been simply a melodramatic tale like hundreds of other cowboy stories, the only difference being that here the hero does not survive.

In this story Crane is concerned with showing the chemistry of change in a way more complex than in "The Blue Hotel." There we saw the distance foreshortened between one level of existence and another by a drink. "A Man and Some Others" reveals in detail the intricacies involved in a psychic alteration, but not in any simplistic fashion. When the stranger arrives at the camp of the sheepherder, he is innocent enough to ask him why he doesn't go to get the sheriff. Frightened and repulsed by his initiation into the awareness of the reality of death when he sees the corpse of the Mexican dispatched by Bill during the first encounter, the stranger finds himself in the position of either killing or being killed. At the end of the story he has not become a *completely* different person; he is not comfortable in the midst of the carnage wrought in part by himself. He has in fact not ceased to be frightened: "There he again stood motionless, his mouth just agape and the same stupid glance in his eyes, when all at once he made a gesture of fright and looked wildly about him." [6] Yet we know that he is a very different person from the person we met when he first rode into the sheepherder's camp.

The events of the story are acted out in front of the familiar backdrop of a nature indifferent to the affairs of men. In this desert waste the two men, isolated from the support of social institutions and aliens in an alien universe, are left to work out their destinies alone, dependent solely upon their own resources.

> Finally, when the great moon climbed the heavens and cast its ghastly radiance upon the bushes, it made a new and more brilliant crimson of the camp-fire, where the flames capered merrily through its mesquit branches, filling the silence with the fire chorus, an ancient melody which surely bears a message of the inconsequence of individual tragedy—a message that is in the bloom of the sea, the sliver of the wind through the grass-blades, the silken clash of hemlock boughs.

The sheepherder is to the young stranger a model of conduct. The older man is wily enough to outwit the

Mexicans in the first encounter, and throughout he exercises the sagacity of one experienced in affairs of violence until during the last attack he has the nearly uncontrollable urge to rush the seven attackers. The stranger sternly commands him: "Don't you budge an inch! . . . Don't you budge!" At the beginning of the tale he saw the spectacle of a man, who, given the alternatives of clearing out from an area which he is entitled to occupy or staying to fight against great odds, chooses the latter course. After the last fight "he suddenly felt for Bill, this grimy sheepherder, some deep form of idolatry."

A story which has proved more popular among the anthologizers and one more often mentioned by critics than "A Man and Some Others" is "Five White Mice." Though in my opinion a far inferior story aesthetically, "Five White Mice" contains certain doctrinal elements which seem to indicate the direction of Crane's thought about the time the story was written, 1898. It has also seemed to some to support one facet of Crane's thought which has occurred from time to time in earlier works, the idea that chance governs one's fate.

Structurally the tale falls into two parts, the one ending after the circus, and the other beginning immediately afterward when the New York Kid begins to look for his companions. The first part is the longest, and it is too long. It overbalances the second; it is less interesting and relevant to the main concern of the story. Crane's method of beginning his stories is nearly always the same. He begins with a general description of some kind, gradually narrowing his focus to concentrate on the area most interesting him. Here his focus does not narrow soon enough. Consequently we are left with an overly long section preparatory to the most important one.

Many of the same problems of composition we saw in *Maggie* recur here. In the first section Crane has the problem of describing a barroom scene. The first paragraph tells us that a gambler, a millionaire, a railway conductor, and the agent of a large American syndicate are playing seven-up by the window. The occupations which these men follow have absolutely no relevance to the scene nor to the tale as a whole, yet Crane, attempting to solve the writer's problem of creating a scene involving many people and things, bothers to name their occupations. The next sentence tells us that Freddie, the bartender, "surveyed them with the ironical glance of a man who is mixing a cocktail." Do men always, or even often, glance ironically when mixing cocktails? Later, when the group of men has entered and is noisily gambling, "one of the quiet company playing seven-up at the corner table said profanely that the row reminded him of a bowling contest at a picnic." Even granting that the allusion to the bowling contest is meaningful, why is the man's statement profane? From whose point of view is it profane? What is meant when after the suggestion to gamble for a box at the circus the group of roisterers is "profoundly edified?" These and other such problems of clarity mar "The Five White Mice."

I question the logic behind the implication of the story that the affair with the Mexicans came off well because the New York Kid, the central character, had lost in the dice game and had as a result been sober. Benson, a minor participant, analyzes the relationship and comes to that conclusion. The New York Kid, agreeing with Benson's analysis, assumes that the encounter with the Mexicans would not have ended so well had he been drunk. He feels that in losing at the dice game he did not really lose because his being sober has allowed him a great victory. If the events occurring from his loss of the game to the encounter with the Mexicans have a direct causal connection, then he is not ruled by "the five white mice of chance," but by determinism. If chance prevails, then any number of things could have happened between the one event and the other. There is nothing to indicate that the three would even have met the Mexicans if the New York Kid had gone drinking with his friends. The New York Kid—and Crane as well—assumes that the group would have had the encounter no matter what had happened previously, an assumption antithetical to the logic of chance.

The best part of "The Five White Mice" is the second

section. The time of the section is brief, considerably shorter than the first section. (Another way in which the first overbalances the second.) The encounter with the Mexican consumes more space in pages than the events before it, but the whole affair actually lasts only a very few minutes. The compression of time in this section during which Crane examines the thoughts and reactions of the New York Kid, is an outstanding artistic achievement. The whole section is suspenseful and vivid, a result of Crane's confining the point of view of the affair to that of the New York Kid. The intensity of the scene seems to be less in the events themselves than in the New York Kid's interpretation of them. Crane's ability to evaluate the relative importance of character and event serves him well here as it served him well in "A Man and Some Others" where the crucial conflict was likewise described from a limited point of view.

Yet, despite the impressiveness of this last section, it is a mistake to generalize about Crane's attitudes and opinions at this particular time in his career on the basis of "The Five White Mice." Nowhere else during this time nor at any other did he attempt to say so unambiguously that the affairs of men are governed by chance. Such works written around this time as "The Blue Hotel," "The Monster," "Twelve O'Clock," "Death and the Child," exhibit concerns somewhat different from the central concern of the story about the New York Kid. Consequently we should not feel that any kind of phase in Crane's thinking is represented by this story.

"Twelve O'Clock" is a story about the irony of fate. More interested here in the ironic plot than in character, Crane gives us no insight into the responses of the participants. They act, but since we see the action only from the outside, as an objective observer might see it, we get little sense of the internal workings of characters and hence we are never very involved with any of them. But that is as it should be, given Crane's intentions. Intent on demonstrating the irony of fate, he wanted also to describe the coming of law and order to the West, a prominent theme of several of his Western tales.

The mechanical bird cuckooing over the dead at the end of the tale is a complexly ironic comment on all that has occurred. It points to the fact that the violence which has erupted over a quite inconsequential thing, that it is so odd and foolish that two men should be dead (the townsmen shot down a cowboy who attempted to ride quickly away after the shooting) and another should be a murderer under such trifling circumstances. At the same time it justifies the claims of Jake, who by this time isn't very much interested in proving his claim. It is a death knell both for Placer and for lawlessness in the town. The townsmen have for the first time come to grips with the problem of the obstreperous cowboys and we may be sure that law and order will reign in this town from hence forth.

But complexity is not in itself valuable. The cuckooing bird does not escape being an overly dramatic ending to a melodramatic tale. Big Watson is the stage villain, who has no particular motive for being evil; he just is. He has no private life, but like everyone else in the story, his only existence is that which we see on the page. He is flat like a one-dimensional drawing. At the same time I see no evidence that Crane did not achieve what he intended. Being more interested here in plot than in character, in revealing a theme than delving into his personages, he nearly created a parody of Western melodrama. And he would have, had the final cuckooing in "Twelve O'Clock" not been too complex for melodrama, though on the surface it indeed has the simplicity of melodrama.

"Horses—One Dash" goes nearly to the opposite extreme in that it is almost entirely an examination of character under stress. But the tale has no substance. We leave Richardson, the central character, just as we met him; no apparent change takes place in him. We know nothing of what his fearful experience has meant to him other than that he was badly frightened. The plot is simple, but the title itself suggests the dependence of the tale on its scant plot for interest. Richardson, an American traveler, arrives one evening at a small Mexican village with his Mexican servant. During the night Mexican bandits arrive, who threaten to rob him; they are distracted by the arrival of women. In the early morning Richardson and his servant set out galloping across the plain. The Mexicans pursue. Richardson meets a cavalry patrol and is saved. "Horses—One Dash" describes an experience which actually happened to Crane, a fact proving once again that the truth of literal experience is no necessary guarantee of good fiction.

"The Bride Comes to Yellow Sky" is a jewel of excellence exquisitely carved. Except for "The Open Boat," the purity and clarity of its conception and execution are unparalleled in Crane's work. The awkward phrasing, the faulty diction, the strained, vague metaphor so characteristic of even Crane's work are not present to mar this story. It escapes being simply melodrama because it is in part comic, the tone indicating that the author is not taking his material entirely seriously. It also delves into the characters of Jack Potter and his new bride, revealing to the reader that their lives extend beyond the immediate conflict described in the tale.

The short story among Crane's works most like "The Bride" is one called "Moonlight on the Snow." There a small Western town, intent on making itself respectable, attempts to execute a well-known member of the community, a gambler, who has killed a man in a dispute. The noose is around his neck when a stagecoach appears, out of which emerge a white-haired old gentleman, a beautiful young lady, and two little girls. "And the rough West stood in naked immorality before the eyes of the gentle East." The men are cowed by this vision, so much so that they are undecided about what to do. The gambler tells them that the hanging is off for the moment, and, ordering a bystander to remove the rope, says, "Boys, when you want me, you'll find me in the Crystal Palace." The problem is solved when a sheriff arrives that night with a warrant for the arrest of the gambler—solved in the sense that the townsmen no longer have the problem of hanging this difficult man. The sheriff is Jack Potter of "The Bride," and his deputy none other than Scratchy Wilson.

In both stories the direction of events is altered by the impingement on the disordered West of the order of the more civilized East. Scratchy Wilson and the men who are about to hang the gambler in "Moonlight on the Snow" are making obeisance, not to people, but to the institutions of Western civilization. It is no accident that Scratchy Wilson is the last of the bad men in Yellow Sky, nor that he, in the other story, has become a lawman. These stories, along with "Twelve O'Clock" are fictional descriptions of an historical fact which had a great deal to do with the direction of American history, the closing of the frontier.[7]

"The Bride Comes to Yellow Sky" is also a spoof on the kind of sentimental Western fiction written earlier by Bret Harte and the many lesser writers, who have turned out drivel about the frontier West ever since. We cannot be entirely serious in our attitude toward hero or villain. The awkwardness of Jack Potter and his homely new bride among the luxuries of a parlor car is mildly humorous. Likewise humorous is the contrast between his cowardice about telling the town he is married, his furtive shyness on the train, and his courage in facing, unarmed, the "dangerous" Scratchy Wilson. Scratchy, his back to the wall as civilization threatens constantly to destroy his role, is comical in his decorative shirt and his fancy boots. But even these little details of dress reflect Crane's attitude toward his materials. The references are humorous and at the same time they indicate the extent to which Scratchy's kind is doomed, for the shirt which the badman wears was made on the East Side of New York, and the boots he wears are "the kind beloved in winter by little sledding boys on the hillsides of New England." In the face of encroaching civilization Scratchy is a child; the town is the toy he plays with. "In the presence of this foreign condition [Potter's marriage] he was a simple child of the earlier plains." His time is past. He is an anachronism. And so is Jack Potter, but he has gone farther in coming to terms with the new condition. Most of the humor in the tale stems from Crane's underlying awareness of the incongruity between the men and their changed environment.

"The Bride Comes to Yellow Sky" is perfectly structured. Each section leads brilliantly toward the climax, the confrontation of Jack and Scratchy. The first section of course introduces us to Jack and his bride, and also suggests that he embodies not only the institution of marriage, but the whole force of orderliness as he returns westward in the ornate parlor car in fact to establish order in a disordered town. The drummer, the stranger in town, allows the author to establish the situation which Potter is about to walk into. We learn of the long-standing antagonism between the sheriff and Scratchy Wilson, thus heightening the suspense. The device is an obvious one and not overly obtrusive. In the third section we meet the "villain," seeing precisely what Potter has to face. And in the fourth the conflict is resolved in a way completely consistent with what has gone before. The gradually mounting tension of the tale is a direct result of the arrangement of its material.

The tone of the total work is dual, but not ambivalent. Crane has at least two levels of meaning working here, one serious, the other comical, nearly farcical. He was able to keep them separate in "The Bride" as he was not always able in earlier works. His serious level remains serious, his comic level remains comic. The characters are viewed consistently and objectively in a manner not entirely characteristic of Crane's best work. Too often he becomes so involved with his characters that he is unable to keep them at a proper distance, but this does not always result in serious flaws unless he is unsure of his feelings toward the characters. Then problems arise. No such problems arise here. This is one of the few stories seeming to have beneath it a broad, sympathetic understanding of humanity. There is nothing of the desperate fury, the intense anxiety appearing in the fiction where Crane is too personally involved.

7

On the Sea in an Open Boat

Though "The Open Boat" is of a piece with Crane's major fiction, it stands apart from other works in style, characterization, and tone. In Crane's handling of these elements we see finally fulfilled the potential indicated so many times in his other publications. Only once did Crane fully realize that potential, "The Open Boat" being the high point of his brief career. The fluency of style here, its evenness throughout, gives evidence, especially when compared with the style of Crane's other good pieces, of his having a clear and exact notion of what he was about in executing "The Open Boat." Very few of those infelicitous phrases and inept comparisons occurring in nearly all of Crane's work appear here. One reason they do not occur is that his feelings toward his characters are settled as well as are his feelings about the total situation. He does not find it necessary to retreat from these characters by treating them ironically, thus turning them into objects, into beings whose humanity he does not grant. This implies a consistency of tone nearly unparalleled in Crane's major fiction. Only once is there a serious lapse of tone: when the reporter lies down in the cold water in the bottom of the boat, the author says "his teeth played all the popular airs." A small thing, nonetheless it disturbs the sympathetic bond existing between reader and character and author and character. It is not unsuitable because it is humorous, but because of the ironic quality of its humor. The phrase is noteworthy since it recalls the frequently recurring tendency which Crane has to be humorous at the expense of his characters, very often when such humor serves no aesthetic end.

"The Open Boat" is the furthest development of a theme which interested Crane all through his career, the relationship of man to nature.[1] If we consider the major concerns of his fiction, fear, death, courage, identity, isolation, it becomes clear that these nearly inseparable abstractions are intimately related to his concept of nature, so closely related in fact that we can say that his concern with them stems from his conclusions about the relationship between man and nature. In Crane's fiction nature has essentially three levels of meaning: it is first of all external, visible nature—trees, rocks, grass, animals. It means also "the laws governing physical phenomena in the universe," those principles regulating the bodily processes, the changes of the seasons, climatic conditions. Finally nature has a metaphysical meaning suggesting the essential character of the universe, of the agency responsible for the operation of the laws of nature, in short, God.[2]

At the very end of "The Open Boat" the three survivors of the harrowing sea adventure feel that they can be interpreters of the voice of the great sea. But what precisely will they interpret, and how will they interpret? Obviously when they interpret the voice of the sea, they will interpret all nature, nature in all of its manifestations. Because the story expands beyond the plight of four men in a boat, it demands that its conclusions be expanded beyond the immediate tale. In interpreting the voice of the sea the three men will be able to talk about man's relation to nature and his relation to other men as a result of his condition.

The surface level of nature in this story, external, visible nature, allows the three men, especially the reporter, he being the protagonist, to make inferences about the other two levels of meaning inherent in the total concept. At the beginning of the story the "waves were most wrongfully and barbarously abrupt and tall, and each froth-top was a problem in small-boat navigation." [3] At the end of the story "the white waves paced to and fro in the moonlight." A great deal has happened between the two points in time, more than simply a change in the weather. It is aesthetically fitting that the sea should be a rough, perilous sea at the opening of the story where it is important that the precariousness of the situation of the characters be emphasized. Similarly it is fitting that at the end of the story, after the reader has followed the characters through their adventure, the sea be calm and apparently docile, at least in comparison with its appearance at the beginning of the story. Just as the fears of the characters have been allayed once they have been saved, so are the fears for them experienced by the reader. The moods and attitudes of the reporter in the boat are not consistently reflected by the state of the sea, but there is some relationship between the author's description of the sea and the attitude of the reporter toward it. The reporter is the only one of the four men whose attitudes toward man and nature undergo a sea change, at least he is the only one we see changing. Perhaps the last line of the story (". . . they felt they could then be interpreters") suggests that all are different after their ordeal, but we don't in fact know the nature of the changes experienced by the others. At the beginning of the story the sea is described as having the conscious intention of swamping the dinghy, of drowning the four men. The waves are "wrongfully and barbarously abrupt and tall" as though consciousness of some kind were working against them. Being in the boat is compared to riding a bucking broncho. Carrying the analogy further, we see that the intention of the bucking broncho is to unseat its rider just as the sea seemingly attempts to unseat the four men. Every wave is "just as nervously anxious to do something effective in the way of swamping boats" as every other. "It was not difficult to imagine," we are told, "that this particular wave was the final outburst of the ocean, the last effort of the grim water." The crests of the waves "snarl" as though expressing hostility toward the passengers of the boat. In the second section of the story sea gulls are near the boat. They appear "uncanny and sinister in their unblinking scrutiny" of the men, and are somehow "gruesome and ominous." As observers we know the sea is in fact not hostile, that the sea gulls are not actually gruesome and ominous. But the men in the boat have this to learn. After the two opening sections of the story the references to the sea as hostile are few and scattered until the final section of the story where they disappear altogether despite the fact that there are enough descriptions of the sea in which Crane could have included such references had he chosen to do so. That he no longer describes the sea as hostile reflects not only on the theme, but on the point of view as well, a matter to be later discussed.

A number of the figures of speech involving images drawn from nature make comparisons with land animals or objects. The waves seen against the horizon appear like jagged rocks. The bucking broncho comparison in the first section is a long extended metaphor comparing the ride in the boat to a wild ride on a horse. The snarling waves suggest a land animal of any kind that snarls. The crest of each wave is a hill. The sea gulls are like prairie chickens, and "it is easier to steal eggs from under a hen than it was to change seats in the dinghy." These figures drawn from external nature serve to broaden the scope of the tale. What the men know at the end of the tale they learn from the sea, but the lesson is a lesson about the whole of life, about man's relation to man and to nature on land or on the sea.

The second level of nature, that involving the operation of the laws governing physical phenomena in the universe, occurs of necessity in any story simply because we are, by the fact of our existence, our physiological makeup, confined within certain limitations. Like all other things in the world we are subject to the laws of gravity, to the laws governing falling bodies, and so forth. Ordinarily we pay little attention to such considerations, largely because the operation of these laws is taken for granted. But in much of Crane's work the case is different. He directs our attention to nature in general and to this particular facet of nature having to do with its workings. He does so because he feels that man, in order to realize his fullest potential, must be free. He becomes free through the exercise of consciousness, will, against the nonconscious forces of nature, which by virtue of their impersonal operation constrain him.

In "The Open Boat," as elsewhere, the antagonist in the story is apparently external nature. However, it is not only visible external nature threatening the men in the boat. Their survival depends likewise on their ability to withstand the nearly unendurable physical torture brought about by their struggle, as well as on their ability to manipulate the boat properly in the face of fatigue and ever-impending catastrophe. They are fatigued because they have not had sufficient rest and nourishment, and because they have had to put forth tremendous physical exertion in order to maintain control of the boat. The state of their bodies is explainable in terms of physiological principles just as the activity of the sea can be explained in terms of the operation of winds and tides, in terms of geophysical principles. Against the operation of all these forces over which they have no control they pit their will to endure.

Since we learn in the story that nature does not in any conscious manner direct hostility toward men, we might expect to find instances in the story where nature's operation is as helpful as it has been hindering. And so we do. When the men use the captain's overcoat as a sail, the wind cooperates quite nicely and they make steady progress over the waves without the necessity, for a while, of rowing. Seemingly stationary mats of brown seaweed allow the men to mark their progress toward the land. At the time the captain needs a stick to make a signal flag he finds one floating near the boat. Near the end of the story, when the reporter is caught in a current, a wave comes along and frees him from the immediate danger, the same wave, possibly, which drowned the oiler.

A third remove from external, visible nature is nature as the manifestation of God. Crane does not discuss God directly in his fiction as he does in his poetry, yet one is likely to feel the presence in the fiction of those attitudes toward God explicitly expressed in much of his poetry. The poetry reveals that Crane never forgave God for allowing natural evil. His blasphemy stemmed from his awareness of the pain and suffering in the world, pain and suffering toward which God seemed indifferent. He was not an atheist.[4] How inconsistent it would be for an atheist to rail against God as Crane does in his poetry. Crane talks about God in his fiction in the only way his materials would allow him to—by talking about nature. When he discusses fictionally the relationship between man and nature, he is in effect discussing the relationship between man and God, for what meaning does it have to attribute attitudes of any kind to nature in and of itself? I do not mean to suggest that Crane identifies nature and God; they are by no means equivalent. But in Crane's thinking God is responsible for the character of nature. Hence man's relationship to His work (nature) is indicative of man's relationship to Him. The benevolence, hostility, or indifference of nature is the benevolence, hostility, or indifference of God. Crane relates the two quite explicitly at the end of *The Red Badge*, where, in one of the deleted passages, Henry feels: "He was emerged from his struggles with a large sympathy for the machinery of the universe. With his new eyes, he could see that the secret and open blows which were being dealt about the world with such heavenly lavishness were in truth blessings. It was a deity laying about him with the bludgeon of correction."

To be sure, when a character in the fiction interprets nature as being either benevolent or hostile, he is seeing with a distorted view. It is clear enough that Henry was mistaken when he felt, "Nature was a fine thing moving with a magnificent justice. The world was fair and wide and glorious. The sky was kind, and smiled tenderly, full of encouragement, upon him." Likewise, when in "The Blue Hotel" the Swede felt so at home in nature that he could say, "Yes, I like this weather. I like it. It suits me," he too sees as through an eye jaundiced. Both project an

inadequate, limited, and entirely personal view onto nature. They cannot properly know their relationship to
others and to the universe at large until they are able to
interpret nature accurately. "The Open Boat" shows how
one man, the reporter, through direct experience with
nature, learns to interpret it truly. Several references in
this tale point clearly toward metaphysical matters. The
thrice repeated refrain is the most obvious reference. "If I
am going to be drowned—if I am going to be drowned—if
I am going to be drowned, why, in the name of the seven
mad gods who rule the sea, was I allowed to come thus far
and contemplate sand and trees?" I suspect that Crane
had no particular deities in mind when he referred to "the
seven mad gods who rule the sea," but meant only to
suggest some agency, metaphysical in character, responsible, at least in the eyes of the reporter, for the predicament of the men. This agency, the reporter feels, has
allowed him to come within sight of safety only to snuff
out his life before he reaches land. He has not simply been
"allowed" to come thus far, but has in fact, we learn in
the next line, been "brought" within sight of safety. The
refrain, we might reasonably conclude, suggests that the
agency which seems to the men responsible for their predicament is fate, especially since after the refrain occurs
for the first time, Fate is explicitly named. The third time
the refrain is repeated, its meaning is somewhat altered by
its context. Judging from the lines following the refrain,
we will likely conclude that the fate alluded to before
becomes at this point a more complex fate.

> During this dismal night, it may be remarked that a man
> would conclude that it was really the intention of the seven
> mad gods to drown him, despite the abominable injustice
> of it. . . .
> When it occurs to a man that nature does not regard
> him as important, and that she feels she would not maim
> the universe by disposing of him, he at first wishes to throw
> bricks at the temple, and he hates deeply the fact that there
> are no bricks and no temples. Any visible expression of
> nature would surely be pelleted with his jeers.

Then, if there be no tangible thing to hoot, he feels, perhaps, the desire to confront a personification and indulge in pleas, bowed to one knee, and with hands supplicant, saying, "Yes, but I love myself."

A high cold star on a winter's night is the word he feels that she says to him. Thereafter he knows the pathos of his situation.

No longer does fate threaten to destroy the men in the boat, but nature. "Nature" here certainly does not mean external, visible nature, for surely the sea is there to be jeered as a visible expression; nor does "nature" mean the laws governing physical phenomena, for visible nature manifests nature's laws. If whatever is to be addressed, to be pled to has existence at all, its existence must be transcendent, it must have intelligence, and it must be, in the mind thinking the above, responsible for the precariousness of the situation of the men in the boat. In short, nature here means God, and to the men in the boat, who despite His indifference desire to live, He is like "a high cold star," unfeeling and aloof from the affairs of men. This becomes even more clear in the final passage dealing directly with the problem of the relation of the men in the boat to nature, a passage detailing the thought of the reporter about the meaning of the situation of the open boat. From the boat the reporter sees a windmill on the shore.

> This tower was a giant, standing with its back to the plight of the ants. It represented in a degree, to the correspondent, the serenity of nature amid the struggles of the individual—nature in the wind, and nature in the vision of men. She did not seem cruel to him then, nor beneficent, nor treacherous, nor wise. But she was indifferent, flatly indifferent.

In the next line we learn that one having this perception is "impressed with the unconcern of the universe." The analogy of the first line of this passage likens nature to an indifferent giant. "Nature" here means first of all external, visible nature ("nature in the wind"). It also means "nature in the vision of men," or as a manifestation of God,

for what is nature in the *vision* of men but this? Further-
more, "nature" here could hardly refer to the system of
laws governing physical phenomena in the universe, for
how meaningful would it be to characterize a law of
physics as "indifferent"? Isn't indifference inherent in the
term itself, the idea of a "benevolent" physical law being a
contradiction in terms? The tower is not simply "a giant,
standing with its back to the plight of the ants." It is God,
standing with his back to men. To be "impressed with the
unconcern of the universe" is to be convinced that no
benevolent agency rests at the center of the cosmos. Man
is alone, Crane says here as elsewhere, an alien in an alien
universe, and having to depend solely on his own resources.

The three refrains occur before the passage quoted
above about the indifference of nature, and are the unartic-
ulated feelings of the four men in the boat. The last
statement about the predicament of the men is an insight
occurring only to the reporter and representing not a
contradiction in Crane's view of nature, but a reassess-
ment on the reporter's part of his relation to nature.
Neither fate nor nature has a desire to dispose of him as
the refrain implies they do; no agency has allowed him to
come as far as he has. Nature is indifferent, showing
neither favor nor disfavor. This insight allows him to
accept the death of the oiler in the end without bitterness.
Nature or fate has not snuffed out the best, the strongest
of them, but *one* of them, and it might have been any
one.[5]

8

Four Minor Novels

In certain respects *The Monster* is the most ambitious piece Crane ever attempted. No other story is as broadly critical of society, nor is there any other work portraying in such realistic detail the life and character of a whole town. Usually Crane's concern is with depicting individuals whose problems are mostly private rather than social in nature. We often get a sense of the presence of society, but the makeup of the large social group is either impressionistically rendered or otherwise suggested. Here numerous townspeople are portrayed individually, each of whom has a part in forming the social attitudes of the town. By no means, however, has Crane forsaken his primary interest in the plight of the individual. Despite the larger canvas, here too his greatest concern is with an individual, one whose values come into conflict with those of the social body. This is the point at which *The Monster* touches Crane's major interests in his other fiction. How will the individual fare who stands alone, facing great odds and having only his own internal strength to rely on? The larger problem explored in the short novel is a perennial one: the man of principle faced with either compromising, thereby gaining certain pragmatic goals, or strictly maintaining his principles and relinquishing more worldly values. The particular circumstances under which this larger problem occurs suggests a theme especially relevant to our time and one indicating a great deal of insight and awareness, be it conscious or not, on Crane's part: the relationship between white and Negro in modern society.

There is no development in the character of Trescott; he goes through no torment deciding what his course of action should be. His character is delineated in the beginning of the story where he firmly, but lovingly, disciplines his son for breaking a flower in the carefully tended yard. He goes about his business with the calm self-assurance of one who never doubts the truth or validity of his own values. He never seems particularly angered by the reactions of the townspeople. Unhesitatingly he goes about doing what he feels he must.

Unless I am over-reading, and in all honesty I admit that possibility, Trescott is intended to be Christlike in character. It seems to me that the analogy is suggested by Crane himself in bringing the name John Twelve into the story. "Twelve" is a very unusual name. "John" attached to it is likely to send a thoughtful person to the Bible, even a person aware of the dangers involved in drawing parallels between that highly symbolic and connotative work and other works of literature. What we find in Chapter 12 of "St. John" is a continuation of the story of Lazarus, whom Jesus raised from the dead. The chapter tells about the chief priests' wanting to be rid of Lazarus, and about the blindness of the Jews who will not believe in Him. In Bethany where a feast is prepared for Christ, "Lazarus was one of them that sat at the table with Him." Coincidence? Possibly but not probably when we consider Judge Hagenthorpe's remarks (in *The Monster*), "He is dead. You are restoring him to life." [1] Obviously Trescott is not Christ; he embodies some of the attributes of Christ though not all; he is not divine, nor is he intended to be.

It is unfortunate that Crane chose to point out this parallel in the way that he did. Naming a character "John Twelve" amounts to pointing outside the story to another object which should supply meaning to the work. He might just as well have added a footnote at the beginning of the story directing the reader to the Lazarus story.

Beyond the character of Dr. Trescott, the story has broad implications involving his relationship with Henry. It is significant that Henry is a monster, faceless, and a black man, who, when freed from the confines of his social and economic position, becomes a frightful menace to society. Before Henry has lost his face and his mind, he has seemed safe to those around him, a recognized, though subservient, member of the general community. But when as a result of his insanity he is no longer restrained by the customs of the country, he becomes like some frightful and terrifying apparition embodying the deepest fears of the community. Henry *seems* to Whilom-ville to be what Bigger Thomas in Richard Wright's *Native Son* actually is: a monster created by his condition as a Negro in America. Henry is in fact harmless. It is only in the clouded eyes of the community that he is a threat, a threat to the Negroes of the town as well. He threatens them because they too fear this man unconstrained by the rigid system of manners which Crane shows Henry partici-pating in prior to his derangement and disfiguration.

But despite the racial theme, which may strike us as especially significant today, *The Monster* is finally a story about human responsibility. If Henry Johnson is a mon-ster, he is only so because he has been made one. The desire of the community to be rid of him, to get him out of sight, is the desire to recognize no responsibility for the man. Only Trescott knows that he is responsible for this "monster," this monster who cannot and will not go away. On this level the final resolution of the story is predeter-mined. Dr. Trescott has no other alternative: he is tied to his creation as a dancer is tied to her dance.

Only one other person in the story, Martha Goodwin, recognizes the human responsibility involved, understand-ing, by implication, why Trescott acts as he does. Interest-ingly enough, another Martha is the person who serves Christ's feast at Bethany in John 12:1. It is Martha Good-win who speaks in favor of Dr. Trescott when her sister and a neighbor present the attitude of the town. "You can't go against the whole town," they tell her. " 'The whole town,' " she echoes. "I'd like to know what you call 'the whole town.' Do you call these silly people who are scared of Henry Johnson 'the whole town'?" But ironically, she alone of the townspeople is treated with singular derision. Prior to her defense of Trescott, she has been presented as the town busybody, a gossip, who has been hardened to life by the early death of her betrothed. "In regard to social misdemeanors, she who was the mausoleum of a dead passion was probably the most savage critic in town." "Serves him right if he was to lose all his patients," she said of Dr. Trescott. What are we to think of an opinion expressed by such a person as she?

It is hard to know, for the ambivalence of Crane's attitude toward her makes evaluation difficult. The tone with regard to her likewise makes difficult the ascertaining of Crane's final attitude toward Trescott. He has led us to believe that her attitudes and opinions are not reliable, resulting as they do from her being "the mausoleum of a dead passion." Her conflicting attitudes represent the same kind of tonal difficulty which occurred in Crane's work earlier. But here the problem is not such a great one, for he has managed to maintain a consistent attitude toward Trescott throughout. I suspect that the presentation of Martha's character suggests Crane's reservations about the doctor's decision to follow the dictates of his conscience rather than to act pragmatically.

The Monster is the best of the four novels dealt with in this section. Its problems are significant and are sufficiently well defined through the action of the tale. A reader might wish better acquaintance with the character of Dr. Trescott, whose apparently single-minded response to his situation suggests that the choice which he makes is easier than it would probably be for most people. Yet we have some indication that his course is not an easy one; the last scene of the piece, where he tries to comfort his wife after she has been snubbed by her former friends, reveals only the beginning of the continual suffering he will undergo as a consequence of defying the will of his social group. Worthy of note also is the insight Crane shows in saying in the tale that this "monster" cannot be locked up in a little room, sent away to an asylum, pushed out of consciousness; that he is a present reality and must be recognized as such. None of the others of these novels approaches the complexity of *The Monster* nor deals with its materials in as satisfying a manner.

The worst of the four novels is *The Third Violet*, a piece about which even Crane's warmest admirers have been unable to speak favorably.[2] In one copy Crane himself inscribed, "This book is even worse than any of the others." [3]

The novel was an attempt to appeal to a popular audience. It was written quickly, most of it being done in November and December of 1895. Crane made little attempt here in either style or subject matter to depart from the conventions of the popular fiction of his day. Consequently it does not contain his characteristic irony, nor, since it is mostly dialogue, do we see many of the figures of speech typical of Crane. Never having succeeded when he attempted to write about love, Crane had even less chance when he wrote superficially about the relationship between the sexes. Miss Fanhall, the stock heroine and proper object of affection for decent, upright men, is so insubstantial as to threaten to disappear from the page. Florinda, the evil and sinful creature, suffers the fate of her kind in the sentimental novel of the nineteenth century. She is punished for having a body. "She has a beautiful figure—beautiful," an artist comments about her. But Miss Fanhall has no body; she does not participate in a world where bodies have any significance. Florinda is the more credible of the two. It is unfortunate that Crane's formula requires that she suffer.

A novel better than *The Third Violet* despite the fact that it has many of the same defects as the earlier work is Crane's *Active Service*,[4] the action of which occurs during the Greco-Turkish war. Though again it seems that Crane was making a bid for popular favor, he was more successful in writing a novel in which the central concerns are not so entirely divorced from those manifested in his other works. He seems to have been more interested here in at least filtering the romance through his own sensibilities, thus creating a story which seems sincere and honest; less

sentimental and hollow than the earlier one about roman-
tic love. However, it should be borne in mind that being a
better novel than *The Third Violet* does not make *Active
Service* a good one. It isn't. Besides incorporating some of
the worst elements of popular fiction, *Active Service* is
stylistically unsound. Were one not familiar with the facts
about its date, he might well conclude that the work was
early rather than late.[5] Many of the problems of style
encountered by a reader in the early fiction reappear here.
Another basic difficulty is in the conception of the central
character, who during the course of the novel oscillates
between being an experienced man of the world and a
college boy. Coincidence plays a great part in the action:
chance meetings occur all to frequently. Despite these
serious limitations the novel manages to escape in part the
inanity of *The Third Violet* because of two factors: the
character of the antagonist, Nora Black, who plays a large,
significant role; and the insight exhibited by Crane, which
allowed him to delve beneath the surface of the convention and discover something of the truth of human experience lurking there.

Nora Black—the name "Black" is intended to describe
her moral character—has her antecedent, in Crane's
fiction, in Florinda O'Connor of *The Third Violet*.[6] She is
one of a host of similar characters in nineteenth-century
American fiction, chief among them being De Forest's
Mrs. Larue, in *Miss Ravenel's Conversion from Secession
to Loyalty*, Hawthorne's Miriam, in *The Marble Faun*,
Hester Prynne, in *The Scarlet Letter*, and Cooper's Judith
Hutter, in *The Deerslayer*. Like her literary forebears
(Hester excepted), Nora stands in contrast to a character
who is her moral opposite; Marjory Wainwright is the
contrasting character in Crane's novel. In all the cases
suggested above, the "dark ladies" seem without exception
to be more credible fictional personages than their
"golden" foils. Though ultimately I do not know why this
is so, I suspect it has something to do with the fact that
these women in being creatures of passion exhibit more
humanity than their opposites. They are more involved in

life; they are more like us in that they know and cannot escape their knowledge that they are physical beings, faced daily with the fact of bodily existence. Marjory Wainwright, like her sisters in nineteenth-century American literature, has no body, and consequently we are likely to find it difficult if not impossible, to locate her among our acquaintances. We all know people *somewhat* like her, but just how ethereal can a real woman be?

Because "dark ladies" are most often antagonists to male characters in nineteenth-century novels, constituting a threat more or less sexual in nature, they are active characters, and consequently more credible. Nora Black pursues Rufus Coleman, the protagonist; Rufus pursues Marjory; Marjory waits to be caught. Without Nora, *Active Service* might very well be another *Third Violet*. In the latter novel the protagonist is not really threatened by Nora's counterpart, Florinda. That novel has no clearly defined antagonistic element, which is another reason for its failure. But in *Active Service* the wicked woman poses a problem not so easily solved, for she is strong-willed, bent on having her own way, and at the same time she elicits an initially strong libidinal response from Rufus. Thus the central problem of the novel revolves about the struggle within Rufus Coleman between desire and duty, between fulfilling his "baser" wants and acting according to his code of morality.

It has been tempting for critics to see *Active Service* as a novel about heroism, but this is not basically true. The problem arises because of the situation Coleman finds himself in: he is in the position of rescuer. Prior to his arrival in Greece, Coleman, like Henry Fleming and the little man of *The Sullivan County Sketches*, time and time again compares himself to the hero of myth and legend, who undergoes great danger in rescuing a fair lady. This fairy-tale motif naturally leads one to believe that the plot primarily concerns heroism, the exercise of courage. But closer examination reveals a number of difficulties arising if the novel is viewed in this way. At the end Coleman is as fearful as he was at the beginning. That is, nothing happens which suggests a resolution of this problem. Before Coleman meets the Wainwright party on the dark road, he is extremely frightened. He loses his fright only when he discovers that the people behind him are friends. They view him as a savior, whereas he is explicitly aware that he is only playing a role, and a patently false role. "He knew that it was the most theatric moment of his life. . . . it occurred to him that his position was ludicrously false, but, anyhow, he was glad. . . . However, when he came to consider this proposition he knew that on a basis of absolute manly endeavor he had rendered her [Marjory] little or no service." If the novel were about courage or heroism, this would be the central episode. However, it occurs in the twelfth chapter, one-third of the way through, and does indeed arise from the fairy-tale motif preceding it. Two hundred pages follow, and only one of the succeeding chapters, the twenty-first, can be construed as relating to the exercise of physical courage. There Coleman and the college students are involved in a brawl with a group of Greeks. Coleman is more frightened than anyone else. Nothing is made of the matter of fear of physical destruction; the problem has no resolution of any kind.

The plot structure reveals the real concern of this piece. The "rescue" of the Wainwright party is in actuality only part of the rising action. There are two climaxes occurring during the course of the events; one is within Coleman when he is on the very verge of being seduced, yet withdraws in time after Nora asks whether she is as nice as Marjory. "It was as if the silken cords had been parted by the sweep of a sword. Coleman's face had instantly stiffened and he looked like a man suddenly recalled to the ways of light." The other climax comes about in the external world when he publicly repudiates Nora, who has quite consciously attempted to convince the Wainwrights that she and Coleman are on very intimate terms. These two events make possible the resolution of the problem raised in the early chapters, the union of Marjory and Rufus in the face of parental opposition, and in the face of a greater antagonistic force, Nora Black, whose sexuality threatens to turn Coleman from his duty.

We are not as far away from *The Sullivan County Sketches* and *The Red Badge* as it might appear, nor from such stories as "The Five White Mice," "Death and the Child," "A Man and Some Others," as well as several other stories where Crane is concerned with the value of consciously controlled activity as opposed to instinctive response. The similarity exists because in *Active Service* Crane explores another facet of the general problem of the development of consciousness away from instinctive, unwilled, nonconscious response. Coleman sees Nora as threatening to consciousness, as one who would destroy him by bending his will to hers. Overhearing her talk with a group of admirers at one point in the novel, Coleman compares it to the song of the sirens, he, by implication, becoming Ulysses, who, had he not lashed himself to the mast of his ship, would have been lured to his death. "Her voice sank to the liquid siren note of a succubus." The comparison seems very appropriate, for Ulysses' problem at this point, insofar as it has to do with resisting those forces hostile to consciousness, is the same as Coleman's. That his real battle is with Nora is suggested by the many references describing their relationship in terms of war. When he makes a mistake in dealing with her, it is a "tactical" error. When she convinces the others that Coleman and she are on intimate terms, she has "won a great battle." Once in the novel he has the great desire to attack her physically. Earlier he said he "had come out to fight with giants, dragons and witches." Coleman finally defines his position as cowardly, but his cowardice is moral, not physical. After he has publicly repudiated her, he feels as Henry Fleming might well have felt: "If I had charged Nora's guns in the beginning they would have turned out to be the same incapable artillery. Instead of that he had run away and continued to run away until he was actually cornered . . ." Having finally overcome this woman who seems to him to threaten destruction of his consciousness, he is now free to unite with Marjory, the friendly spirit, to whom he can submit without fear.

If *Active Service*, to the degree to which it adheres to a formula, tends to falsify reality by oversimplifying it, then

The O'Ruddy falsifies and distorts even more. It is a swashbuckling romance about an Irishman, who, through daring feats of arms, wins his ladylove. Though not to be taken seriously, the novel has about it the charming appeal of the well-executed adventure tale. Anyone approaching it seriously, in the manner demanded by others of Crane's works, is bound to come away disappointed. But the reader who finds it possible to suspend his desire for seriousness is likely to discover an extremely amusing, satirical tale possessing as much merit as a novel of its kind can possess, and more merit than most of its kind because it refuses to take itself seriously. Thus its distortions are bearable since the author never himself forgets, nor allows the reader to forget, that novels of its kind are not serious works.

Certain problems arise in treating this novel as though Crane were its sole author. At his death it remained unfinished, he having completed only about one-fourth of it. He personally requested Robert Barr, a former neighbor at Ravensbrook in England, a friend and novelist, to finish the manuscript, a job which Barr undertook with the greatest reluctance, in part because he felt unsuited to handle the task, and in part because he didn't have much faith in the work. Naturally Barr had to make the style of the whole narrative uniform. Consequently, Crane is not visible in the result. The humor is more subtle than Crane's humor usually is. Only one other piece of Crane's is written in a similar tone, "Ol' Bennet and the Indians." More knowledge about people and customs in eighteenth-century England is exhibited here than I would suspect Crane had. Barr apparently had a thorough knowledge of the social history of the time.

It seems that Barr tried as best he could to follow the line of development indicated by that part of the manuscript Crane finished, as well as to follow the directions Crane gave for the remainder of the book. Be this as it may, *The O'Ruddy* is not Crane's work. As the novel stands, and given its intentions as it stands, Crane could not possibly have written it so well. Only the basic conception is his.

9

Crane's Fiction: An Overview

There is a certain sense in which Crane is the least consistent of writers, a fact to be pointed out, not as implying a negative value judgment, consistency in itself being no virtue, but as the great stumbling block constantly befuddling the critic who wishes to trace a clear line of development from *The Sullivan County Sketches* to *The O'Ruddy*. Crane is elusive in this respect. His career cannot conveniently be divided into phases without a significant degree of distortion, without ignoring some factors, overemphasizing others. His attitudes and ideas about himself and about his world were never settled. Consequently we find him frequently altering his style, not in any controlled way, but at random, sometimes writing this way, sometimes that, sometimes reaching back to an earlier style, sometimes creating a new one. Often, most often, in fact, even individual works will not maintain stylistic consistency. When this occurs, aesthetic problems arise. In any case both his shifting perspective on the world and his frequently changing style are in part responsible for the feeling one gets in reading all of Crane's fiction, that he is constantly involved in experimentation.[1]

The works of most authors, certainly major authors, have a greater degree of unity than Crane's because of several rather obvious reasons. His fiction does not take place in any particular region or country. It does not generally deal with broad types of characters. Some of it is not intended to be serious. Some of his work is midway between reportorial writing and light fiction. The range of quality of his published work is greater than that of most good authors, some being very good and some being embarrassingly bad. In notably few instances can we say that he was involved with particular themes or subjects at particular times during his career; he was likely to write about any one of his themes at any time. Though there certainly must have been development between *Maggie* and "The Open Boat," it is no clearly defined development. The essential difference between these two works—at least in terms of the quality of their writing—seems to me a difference in Crane's attitude toward his material rather than a great increase in technical skill. His techniques improved to some degree, but the critic who explains Crane's career in developmental terms has a great deal of explaining to do when he sees Crane making many of the same errors in *Active Service*, a late piece, that he made in *The Red Badge* and even in *Maggie*, errors which he managed to avoid in some of the intervening pieces.

Very often Crane's attitude toward his material as revealed by his tone accounts for qualitative differences among his best works. Many of his light pieces, those having little thematic significance, are not beset with problems of tone. But when he dealt with his innermost concerns, problems of tone almost invariably arose. This suggests, and I believe it to be actually the case, that all too frequently Crane failed to achieve sufficient aesthetic distance between himself and his materials. In *Maggie* it would seem that he is all too distant, but his distance from his characters there is not aesthetic distance; it is not a sufficiently disinterested distance, for his emotional involvement with those characters, negative though it may be, is much too great to allow the objective relation that must exist between artist and art. *George's Mother* finds him too much in sympathy with Mrs. Kelcey, and too little with George. His ambivalent feelings toward Henry Fleming nearly destroy that novel where he (Henry) appears. Likewise Crane does not achieve sufficient aesthetic distance from the Swede in "The Blue Hotel." He bears consistent malice toward him, a great error since it deprives the Swede of his humanity, making it impossible for the reader to recognize him as representing mankind, as Crane intends. In "The Bride Comes to Yellow Sky" problems of tone do not arise, because it does not involve Crane's innermost feelings. He does not take Scratchy or the Sheriff seriously, and there is never any doubt on the reader's part about whether he should view them seriously. "The Open Boat" also suggests that Crane's attitude toward his materials is well under control. Except in one or two minor instances he manages to sustain a consistently sympathetic attitude toward his characters, never viewing them as fools whose opinions should be doubted because they are fools. Even when the protagonist, the correspondent, interprets nature wrongly—seeing it as actively hostile—he is not treated with the devastating irony which Henry Fleming is subjected to when he interprets wrongly. In "The Open Boat" there is an underlying compassion for humanity seldom found in Crane's fiction.

The varying degrees of personal involvement which Crane had with his characters affected his style so much as to elicit from nearly anyone reading the corpus of his work the feeling that Crane is the least consistent of authors. In Hawthorne and Melville, in James, Hemingway, and Faulkner one perceives a central, a core attitude toward their materials which, despite the varying styles of individual works, produces the effect of an over-all uniformity. This core of attitude is missing from Crane's work as a whole. We saw in *Maggie* that the distance between the formal manner of speaking of the narrator and the sub-literate manner of the Bowery inhabitants is a measure of the antipathy felt by the author toward his characters, indicating the intimate relationship between style and tone. Such works as *The Third Violet* and *Active Service*, in large part because of their styles (though of course because of theme and subject matter as well), almost seem to have been written by a different author from the author of *Maggie*. Whereas the style of the earlier novel suggests Crane's hatred of his characters, the style of *The Third Violet* indicates a regard for its characters so great as very nearly to idealize them out of existence. Likewise his tone in dealing with Marjory Wainwright and Rufus Coleman, as revealed through style, suggests a too great involvement with his characters. Compare his feelings toward the people in any one of these works with those expressed in "The Open Boat," "The Bride Comes to Yellow Sky," or even "An Episode of War." In these the characters are treated with much greater artistic objectivity. A consistency of style and tone exists among these last named, which is not to be found in Crane's work as a whole.

If we find Crane's total production to be so varied that it lacks the kind of consistency found among the writings of a great many other authors, we will at the same time find certain larger consistencies existing at least in his serious pieces. Were we to trace to their source the central topics of most of his serious fiction, we would discover that they all lead to one large problem, the problem of identity. Crane wrote about death, courage, isolation, fear, war, the child-parent relationship, brotherhood, love (in *Active Service,* a semiserious work; I exclude *The Third Violet* from consideration here), determinism, nature, and society. No one of these topics occurs in isolation, for they all are related. They ramify from the problem of identity.

I earlier described the process of the achievement of identity in Crane's fiction as the development of consciousness. To Crane "identity" meant the ability to act freely, unconstrained by fear, passion, instinct, parental domination, or social pressure. In order to act freely, one must exercise the powers of consciousness; the degree to which one can act freely is dependent upon the degree to which consciousness is developed. All of Crane's heroes are either involved in the process of the development of consciousness or they show us the sufficiently developed consciousness operating in the world, usually for the better though sometimes for the worse for its possessor and those around him.

The problems Crane's major characters find themselves involved in often reveal the degree to which he was attuned to the pulse of his age. In his fiction he was working out in that form many of the same problems confronting the leading thinkers of the late nineteenth and early twentieth centuries, often coming to similar conclusions. Crane obviously was not a systematic thinker, nor did he intend to be. Yet he articulated in fictional terms a number of the important questions of the age. Like many other thoughtful persons, he was concerned with coming to terms with the conception of man presented by science in the nineteenth century, especially biology. What, asked Crane, is the relationship between man and nature? To what degree is man involved in the processes of nature? Can intelligence, conscious effort, direct events in the world to any meaningful degree? To what extent does Darwin's description of evolution in nature describe man in society? If the conclusions of Darwinism are true, what is the relationship between man and God? These are the larger questions. Their ramifications specifically describe the themes of most of Crane's work.

Another theme linking him to the intellectual climate of his time is the significant matter of the disappearance of the frontier and the impingement on the West of the orderliness of the East. "The Blue Hotel," "Moonlight on the Snow," "Twelve O'Clock," "The Bride Comes to Yellow Sky" are works incorporating in various degrees this theme. Frederick Jackson Turner's explication of the effect on American history of the closing of the frontier, begun only a few years before Crane dealt with the subject, is undoubtedly one of the most important historical theses to be developed during the late nineteenth and early twentieth centuries. Any work on the intellectual history of the era will show relevance to Crane's major themes in his serious fiction.

His importance in the twentieth century has been in part because he was in touch with a great number of the problems which this century has seen as basic. At the same time, he wrote about these issues in a way that distinguishes him as one of the most modern authors. In his employment of language he usually attempted to go beyond the limitations imposed by convention, drawing upon diction either colloquial or formal depending on his experience of language rather than on any established norm. Generally his effort was directed toward completely individual expression, which meant recognizing as few limitations as possible. He wrote often about "unpleasant" things, feeling that in order to depict things as they really are, or as they really might be, the artist should be able to utilize any facet of experience within the range of his imagination. Hence he wrote about a prostitute, about loose women; he incorporated in his fiction the least pleasant aspects of Bowery life, the depravity of its inhabitants and the squalor of their surroundings; he described in great detail people in the process of dying or decaying after death. Violence and bloodshed are not uncommon in Crane's fiction. For good or ill, he was one of those responsible for freeing the modern author from the bounds of tradition and for creating a climate of opinion among the public which would allow the author to exercise such freedom. Because Crane wrote, the range of styles, subject matter, and attitudes a writer might take toward his materials widened so much as to increase immeasurably the possibilities of fiction in the twentieth century.

Crane's fiction undoubtedly contains many serious flaws. I am never surprised when a sensitive reader tells me he finds it difficult to go back to Crane in the way we often return to great writers, finding in them an inexhaustible source of knowledge and pleasure. But if Crane does not hold his own among the greatest American authors, except, perhaps, in the degree of his subsequent influence, we must at least grant that he achieved some things unsurpassed before his time or afterward. There is no greater short story in our literature than "The Open Boat." "The Bride Comes to Yellow Sky" and "The Blue Hotel" are outstanding performances, among the very best of our short fiction. *The Red Badge* is a very good novel, marred by its failure of tone and by the frequent infelicity of its style. These works are the best, and they comprise a very small segment of Crane's total work. But they are enough in my estimation to assure Crane the position of our greatest minor author.

Notes

Introduction

1. *PMLA*, XVII (Winter, 1950), 119–29.

2. The one significant exception to this, the most balanced evaluative judgment yet to appear, is Warner Berthoff's in *The Ferment of Realism: American Literature, 1884–1919* (New York, 1965), pp. 227–35.

3. *Bollingen Series* XLII (New York, 1954).

4. *Ibid.*, p. 43.

5. John E. Hart has used a similar method of interpretation in "*The Red Badge of Courage* as Myth and Symbol," *University of Kansas City Review*, XIX (Summer, 1953), 249–56.

6. In an attempt to avoid the terminology of psychology, I have resisted using terms other than "development of consciousness" and "ego" in the body of this work. Both are justifiable, "development of consciousness" being more adequately descriptive than "achieving maturity" or "manhood," and "ego" having become in its psychological denotation a part of the general vocabulary.

7. I discuss this relation in "Crane's *The Red Badge of Courage*," *The Explicator*, XXIV (Feb. 1966), Item 49.

1 – Crane in the Woods

1. These sketches are light, but certainly not as light as Edwin Cady suggests: "The largest significance of *The Sullivan County Sketches* may be, however, their recording so early and purely the meaning and weight to Crane the artist of the experience of Crane the Sportsman." *Stephen Crane* (New York, 1962), p. 101.

2. Beer early noted Crane's obsession with problems surrounding fear: "Let it be noted that the mistress of this boy's mind was fear. His search in aesthetic was governed by terror as that of other men is governed by the desire of women." Thomas Beer, *Stephen Crane: A Study in American Letters* (New York, 1923), p. 296.

3. This and subsequent quotations from the *Sketches* are taken from Melvin Schoberlin's edition of *The Sullivan County Sketches of Stephen Crane* (Syracuse University Press, 1949).

4. The pattern of retreat into some enclosed, sheltered area occurs time and time again in Crane's fiction. Almost invariably there is an implied contrast between such areas and the world outside. These areas are never satisfactory to the character who finds himself in one; the threat of various dangers within these containing areas serves to thrust the character back into the world.

5. Introduction to *The Sullivan County Sketches*, p. 17. It seems to me that Schoberlin's error stems from his having read later attitudes, those expressed in *Maggie* perhaps, into the earlier fiction. There are naturalistic attitudes expressed here, but not determinism. For as I read these tales, the little man has the potential of dissociating himself from nature through exercise of will. Thus in some of the tales he himself directs the course of events.

6. Time and time again Crane indicates whether a character is in control of himself by reference to the condition of his legs. The device is used frequently in *George's Mother* and in *The Red Badge*, especially in the latter work.

7. This again suggests the inadequacy of Schoberlin's contention that the tales show that the characters are determined.

2—Crane Among the Darwinians

1. Maxwell Geismar implies agreement by saying that Crane's understanding of Darwinism was limited. *Rebels and Ancestors* (Boston, 1953), p. 135.

2. John Berryman, *Stephen Crane*, American Men of Letters Series (New York, 1950), p. 24. Eric Solomon suggests an even longer list but is careful to admit the degree to which he is speculating in *Stephen Crane in England: A Portrait of the Artist* (Ohio State University Press, 1964) pp. 26–28. For other estimates of the extent of Crane's reading see Alfred

Kazin, *On Native Grounds* (New York, 1942), p. 181; James B. Colvert, unpublished doctoral thesis, *The Literary Development of Stephen Crane* (Louisiana State University, 1953), p. 181; Thomas Beer, p. 292; and Edwin Cady, pp. 69–70.

3. See Lars Ahnebrink, *The Beginnings of Naturalism in American Fiction*, Upsala University Essays and Studies on American Language and Literature (Upsala, 1949), p. 11.

4. Philip Quilibet, "Darwinism in Literature," *Galaxy*, XV (1873), 695.

5. Bert J. Lowenberg, "Darwinism Comes to America," *Mississippi Valley Historical Review*, XXVII (Dec. 1941), 341.

6. This view is supported by David Fitelson in "Stephen Crane's *Maggie* and Darwinism," *American Quarterly*, XVI (Summer 1964), 182–94. This article as well as other major articles on *Maggie* is reprinted in Maurice Bassan, ed., *Stephen Crane's Maggie: Text and Context* (San Francisco, 1966).

7. Edward Garnet in *Friday Nights, Literary Criticism and Appreciation* (New York, 1922): "The Bowery inhabitants, as we, can be nothing other than what they are; their human nature responds inexorably to their brutal environment," p. 214.

8. Crane made the same essential inscription in several copies of the book. See R. W. Stallman and Lillian Gilkes, eds., *The Letters of Stephen Crane* (New York, 1960), Nos. 18 (p. 14) and 58 (p. 49). See also 14 n.

9. Compare Walter Sutton, "Pity and Fear in 'The Blue Hotel,'" *American Quarterly*, IV (Spring, 1952), 76. "The very choice of theme and situation indicates an attitude of protest against social injustice which must have sprung from compassion," p. 77. See Notes 11 and 12 below.

10. This and subsequent quotations from *Maggie* are taken from William Gibson's edition of *The Red Badge of Courage and Selected Prose and Poetry* (New York, 1960).

11. Maxwell Geismar agrees: Maggie "is a curiously wooden, graceless and unsympathetic figure when compared with Carrie Meeber or even Trina of *McTeague*," p. 77. William T. Lenehan also agrees in "The Failure of Naturalistic Techniques in Stephen Crane's *Maggie*," Bassan, pp. 166–73.

12. Cf. Oscar Cargill's statement, "He [Crane] is wholly devoid of any sympathy for Maggie, but this comes not from a scientific detachment, rather from ignorance." *Intellectual America*, p. 85.

13. In the same letter Crane writes, "A person who thinks himself superior to the rest of us because he has no job and no pride and no clean clothes is as badly conceited as Lillian Russell." *Letters*, p. 133. Crane's lack of sympathy for slum dwellers is likewise indicated in one of his war dispatches sent from Cuba during the Spanish American War, "Hunger Has Made Cubans Fatalists": "Everyone knows that the kind of sympathetic charity which loves to be thanked is often grievously disappointed and wounded in tenement districts, where people often accept gifts as if their own property had turned up after a short absense." R. W. Stallman and E. R. Hageman, *The War Dispatches of Stephen Crane* (New York, 1964), p. 163.

William Graham Sumner stated this attitude in more extreme terms: "The weak who constantly arouse the pity of humanitarians and philanthropists are the shiftless, the imprudent, the negligent, the impractical, and the inefficient, or they are the idle, the intemperate, the extravagant, and the vicious." "The Forgotten Man," *The Forgotten Man and Other Essays by William Graham Sumner* (New Haven, 1919), p. 475.

14. Berryman disagrees saying that in no American work "had the author remained so persistently invisible behind his creation," p. 59. Cf. Granvill Hicks, *The Great Tradition* (New York, 1933), p. 161. Hicks observes that Crane feels less than kind toward Maggie.

15. XLIV (November 1893), 25.

3 – George's Mother and Other Minor Bowery Works

1. This and subsequent quotations from *George's Mother* are taken from R. W. Stallman's edition of *Stephen Crane: An Omnibus* (New York, 1952).

2. See William York Tindall, *A Reader's Guide to James Joyce* (New York, 1959), pp. 92–93.

3. R. W. Stallman's interpretation of the "red wafer" image is well enough known. The symbolic interpretation of *George's Mother* referred to here appears in *Omnibus*, pp. 19–20.

4. See James B. Colvert and Lars Ahnebrink, p. 65 n. Both agree that George is potentially a free agent, that his problem is primarily internal rather than imposed by his environment.

5. See John Berryman, p. 134 n. Cf. R. W. Stallman, *Letters*, p. 121 n. Stallman corrects the impression that the book was at one time called *Dan Emmonds*.

6. "George drives his mother to her death by drinking. This is the whole open plot of the short novel." Berryman, p. 319.

7. See p. 27 and note 8, Chap 2.

8. This and subsequent quotations from the Bowery works are taken from Wilson Follett's edition of *The Works of Stephen Crane* (New York, 1925–27).

9. Compare Stallman, *Omnibus*, pp. 11–12.

10. This is inferred. The tone and diction of this tale suggest to me that this family is the Johnson family. Nothing in the tale indicates otherwise.

4 – Crane at War: The Red Badge

1. *PMLA*, LXXIII (Dec. 1958), 572. Cf. Wallace Stegner, *The American Novel from Cooper to Faulkner* (New York, 1965). Stegner says what Greenfield says in another way: "Probably he [Crane] intended to have his cake and eat it too—irony to the end, but heroism too," p. 90.

2. This and subsequent quotations from *The Red Badge* are from the edition of William Gibson cited above.

3. Compare Maurice Bassan, "Misery and Society: Some New Perspectives on Stephen Crane's Fiction," *Studia Neophilogica*, XXXV (1963), 104–20. ". . . human courage is by its very nature subhuman; in order to be courageous, a man must abandon the highest of his human facilities, reason and imagination, and act instinctively, even animalistically," p. 194.

4. For examples, William Gibson, ed., *Stephen Crane: The Red Badge of Courage and Selected Poetry and Prose*, 6th printing (New York: Rhinehart and Co., 1960); Richard Lettis *et al.*, eds., Stephen Crane's *The Red Badge of Courage: Text and Criticism* (New York: Harcourt, Brace and Co., 1960); R. W. Stallman, *Omnibus*. There seems to me to be a problem involving proper judgment on the part of the editors who reprint passages expunged by Crane from the completed work. Including within the text itself the material deleted by the author seems to me a betrayal of the author. It

is presumptuous for an editor to add or take away from the text presented by the author for publication and the editor who does so violates the text even if he *thinks* he is performing a useful function. Frederick C. Crews agrees in his edition of the novel (New York, 1964), pp. xxx–xxxi. The editors, Lettis *et al.*, solve the problem by placing deleted passages at the end of the novel, thus evincing consideration for the integrity of the artist's work. Richard Chase, ed., *The Red Badge of Courage* (Boston: Houghton Mifflin, 1960) omits the deletions, but for the wrong reasons. He finds them "inferior to the whole."

5. There are perhaps two minor exceptions. The phrase "with what he thought to be" suggests a disparity between what Henry thought and what Crane thought, in which case Henry here would be simply deluding himself again. In choosing the word "quaint," Crane faintly suggests an ironical attitude whether we interpret the word as meaning "expert," "crafty," or "strange."

6. This distinction reveals that it is not helpful to compare Crane to Chaucer in terms of a "duality of vision" as Stanley Greenfield does in "The Unmistakable Stephen Crane." *PMLA*, LXIII (December, 1958), 562–72.

7. Compare Stallman, *Omnibus*, p. 217. Edwin Cady agrees that the passages deleted from the novel are antithetical to Crane's intentions, at least insofar as they express specifically naturalistic ideas. *Stephen Crane*, p. 126.

8. "Crane's novel has no real 'symbolic' center to which everything else is related. . . . But if it had, I think it would be the great scene in the forest 'chapel,' where the fleeing Henry discovers the decaying corpse." Chase, Introduction to *The Red Badge of Courage*, p. xiv.

9. The function of this character is suggested in a brief paragraph by John E. Hart in "*The Red Badge of Courage* as Myth and Symbol," (Introduction, n. 5) though Hart does not develop this idea.

See my article (Introduction, n. 7) which deals with this character.

10. A figure very much like such figures as these and culturally closer to Crane appears in Nathaniel Hawthorne's "My Kinsman, Major Molineaux." The role of the kind stranger in that tale has been ably discussed by Hyatt H. Waggoner, *Hawthorne, A Critical Study* (Cambridge, 1955), pp. 47–53. Roy R. Male follows Waggoner, amplifying the

implications of the earlier study, *Hawthorne's Tragic Vision* (Austin, Texas, 1957), pp. 48–53. More recently Daniel Hoffman has elaborated further in his richly suggestive *Form and Fable in American Literature* (New York, 1961), pp. 113–25. The concensus of these critics is that the kind stranger in Hawthorne's story serves the essential function of helping Robin along in his progress toward maturity. I am indebted to Professor Waggoner for suggesting this parallel and for directing me to Professor Hoffman's study.

11. Compare Hart, p. 256. Hart believes that "the moral and spiritual strength of the individual springs from the group. . . . [occurs] through the identification of self with group." I consider Henry's reliance on the attitudes and opinions of the group a weakness to be overcome. Donald Pizer appears closer to Hart. "He [Crane] attacks the conventional heroic ideal by showing that a man's actions in battle are usually determined by his imitations of the actions of others—by the group as a whole." *Realism and Naturalism in Nineteenth-Century American Fiction* (Southern Illinois University Press, 1966) p. 30.

12. Heretofore no critic has given sufficient attention to the differing attitudes and reactions of Henry during each of the five encounters. Most commentators have generalized from one or two battles, not apparently realizing that in each encounter Henry is different; not realizing that each battle has a separate function in the novel. For this reason Charles C. Walcutt in his excellent *American Literary Naturalism: A Divided Stream* (Minneapolis, 1956), p. 81, is led to say that Henry's encounter with the opposing force after his return does not reveal an act of courage, but rather a blind animalistic response to threat. The statement is true of the third battle, but since it is not true of the fourth and fifth, it is a faulty generalization. Likewise, Henry should not be described as an "emotional puppet" as Mr. Walcutt describes him. It seems quite evident that this is true only during part of the novel.

5—Some Other Tales of War: Heroism Re-examined

1. Quotations from "The Veteran" are from William Gibson's edition of Crane's work, Chap. 4, n. 4.

2. This and subsequent quotations from the war tales are from the Wilson Follett edition, Chap. 3, n. 8.

3. Of course I distinguish here between Crane's early fili-

bustering adventure which resulted in the experience recorded in "The Open Boat," and his later trip to Cuba as a war correspondent.

6—"The Blue Hotel" and Other Tales of the Woolly West

1. The first part of this chapter first appeared as " 'The Blue Hotel' and the Ideal of Human Courage" in *The University of Texas Studies in Literature and Language*, VI (Autumn, 1964), 388–97.

2. This and subsequent quotations from "The Blue Hotel" are from William Gibson's edition of Crane's work, Chap. 4, n. 4.

3. Charles C. Walcutt, p. 75.

4. Stanley Greenfield, p. 567.

5. *Letters*. No. 213, Joseph Conrad to Edward Garnett, p. 155.

6. This and subsequent quotations from the Western tales are from the Wilson Follett edition of Crane's work, Chap. 3, n. 8.

7. That Crane was concerned with such a theme indicates again the rather surprising fact (surprising in view of the apparent extent of his reading) that his fiction very often deals with matters which the intellectuals of the day were writing and talking about. Frederick Jackson Turner anticipated Crane by only a few years with his thesis delving into the significance of the frontier in American history.

7—On the Sea in an Open Boat

1. Though our interpretations turn out to be quite different, the editors Ray B. West and R. W. Stallman likewise see the relation of man to nature as the central theme of "The Open Boat" in *The Art of Modern Fiction* (New York, 1949), pp. 53–57.

2. A sound, thorough discussion of Crane's attitudes and feelings about God appears in Daniel Hoffman's *The Poetry of Stephen Crane* (New York, 1957), pp. 43–59.

3. This and subsequent quotations from "The Open Boat" are from the edition of William Gibson, Chap. 4, n. 4.

4. Hoffman, p. 66.

5. Compare Stallman, *Omnibus*, p. 418.

8—*Four Minor Novels*

1. This and subsequent quotations from these four novels are from the Wilson Follett edition of Crane's works cited above.

2. Edwin Cady is an exception here. He finds a certain "charm" in the novel, p. 146.

3. *Letters*, R. W. Stallman and Lillian Gilkes, eds., p. 143.

4. H. G. Wells feels that *Active Service* is Crane's worst. *Ibid.*, p. 315.

5. For the facts about the date of *Active Service* see *Ibid.*, p. 146.

6. Maxwell Geismar, p. 112, discusses the women in Crane's fiction, seeing their portrayals as revealing conflicts within Crane.

9—*Crane's Fiction: An Overview*

1. Daniel Hoffman, p. 255. Edwin Cady concurs, p. 46, as does Warner Berthoff, p. 231.

Index

style and theme, xiv; in *George's Mother*, 52; in "The Dark Brown Dog," 55; in *The Red Badge*, 88–89; in shorter fiction, 105; in "The Blue Hotel," 111, 116; in "The Bride Comes to Yellow Sky," 126; in "The Open Boat," 127; in *The Monster*, 139; and style generally considered, 147–49; mentioned, 61

Turner, Frederick Jackson. *See* Frontier

"Twelve O'Clock": chance in, 122, 122–23; irony in, 123; parody in, 123; mentioned, 122, 150

"The Upturned Face": plot of, 103; and *The Red Badge*, 103; subject of, 103–4; mentioned, 100

"The Veteran": structure of, 90–91; compared with *The Red Badge*, 91; theme of, 92; compared with "A Mystery of Heroism," 93; compared with "An Indiana Campaign," 93; mentioned, 100

Waggoner, Hyatt H.: *Hawthorne: A Critical Study*, 158, 159

Walcutt, Charles C.: *American Literary Naturalism: A Divided Stream*, 159; and naturalism in *The Red Badge*, 159

A Woman Without Weapons: original title of *George's Mother* 40, 52

Women: in nineteenth-century American fiction, 141–42

Wright, Richard: *Native Son*, 138